Creating Your Future

Keys to Recognising, Preparing for
and Going for Opportunities

By
Rexford Sam

Published by MediaWorks Global Ltd
www.mediaworksglobal.tv

ISBN 978-1-9999364-0-2 E-Book
ISBN 978-1-9999364-1-9 Paperback

For speaking invitations and consulting engagements,
please send email to **r.sam@rainbowglobal.co.uk**

Disclaimer

The accuracy and completeness of information provided herein and opinions stated herein are not guaranteed or warranted to produce any particular results and the advice and strategies, contained herein may not be suitable for every individual. The author shall not be liable for any consequential, indirect or special loss or damage; neither will he be liable for any loss of profit, income, revenue, anticipated savings, contracts, business, goodwill, reputation, data, or information incurred as a consequence of the use and application, directly or indirectly, of any information presented in this book. This book is designed to provide accuracy in regard to the subject matter covered. The author has used his knowledge, experience, observations and efforts in preparing this book.

Dedication

This reloaded edition is dedicated to those who sometimes feel life is devoid of opportunities for them, to all who need clarity in terms of a sense of direction for their lives, and to those individuals and organisations that want to create a better future.

Acknowledgements

My gratitude to God for His enabling grace to complete this reloaded version of the original publication.

Thanks to Andrew and Sarah Ekuban of Myth Designs for the cover design and to Vike Springs Publishing for the interior design.

I am immensely grateful for the impactful messages and ministry of Pastor Matthew Ashimolowo, Global President and Senior Pastor of Kingsway International Christian Centre (KICC), and the opportunity given me to spearhead the social media ministry.

My sincere thanks to my family - Matilda, Gerald, Charlotte, Charles, Carlien, Josie, Maureen and Levinia for their prayers and support.

I am truly grateful to my friend and coach, Norva Semoy Abiona, for her remarkable insights, candidness and support.

Contents

Introduction

I am reminded of a story about a very religious man who heard on the newscast that a hurricane had been forecast to hit the city he lived in, and as a result, all residents had been asked by the city officials to evacuate at once. This man did not heed the warning, saying to himself that God would save him.

As the storm approached, a police officer knocked on his door and repeated the warning that he should leave right away. The man refused and explained to the police officer that God would save him.

Shortly afterwards, the storm hit, and the surge flooded the city. A rescue worker in a rowboat tapped on the man's second story window and offered him escape. The man yet again refused the help, saying God would save him.

The flood continued to rise, and by nightfall the man had climbed up onto his roof. A helicopter overhead spotted him in its light beam and dropped a rope to the man. He waved them off, shouting back that he did not need help as God would save him.

The flood soon rose above the roofline, and the floundering man drowned.

In heaven, the man demanded to know why God had betrayed him. "I trusted you to save me," he cried, "but you let me drown!"

God answered, "I sent to you a newscast, a police officer, a rowboat, and a helicopter, but you refused all the help I sent!

Having heard the above story, you might be saying to yourself, "A very foolish man."

I do believe in divine interventions because they do happen. Divine interventions, however, do not always come in an earth-shattering manner. Instead, they are often presented as normal events or encounters in our daily life – just like the different types of help offered to the man in the flood story above.

The moral of the story is that we all get presented with opportunities to get out of some dire circumstances and live a better life, but very often we fail to recognise them.

Many therefore unfortunately go through life with struggles, pain, or anxious anticipation of some miracle, like winning a large lottery sum or some divine intervention - eager for a change in their current or worsening circumstances, but never doing anything about it.

This picture seems to be reflected in every society. In interacting with audiences wherever I go, I cannot but notice the yearning to change or improve personal, family or organisational circumstances.

This yearning is often characterised by a restlessness or dissatisfaction with the current state of affairs. Sadly though, many have allowed discouragement to set in because of their perceived incapability to realise their dreams and goals.

This perception is usually due to some seemingly insurmountable barrier or enormous challenge being faced. With the passage of time, frustration set in, leading to either resignation or settling for some mediocre position or route. Some have resorted to quick-fixes to get out of undesirable situations, particularly in dealing with financial challenges or legal situations, which oftentimes have unpleasant consequences.

The above representations, as well as others not specifically mentioned, all point to one thing: all of them want a better future but are uncertain about how to have it. Their waned hopes need to be rekindled.

Hope means *"to look forward to with desire and reasonable confidence. It is the feeling that what is wanted can be had or that events will turn out for the best."*

Hope is that one thing that re-ignites dreams. It leads to the realisation of cherished dreams and to the achievement of life-long goals.

This book will challenge everyone, irrespective of age, financial status, physical condition or personal circumstances - and push organisations too - to the next level.

You probably have been asking if there is any hope in life for you, your family, or your organisation. The good news is that there is definitely hope for the future.

The question to ask then is "How well am I preparing myself for the kind of future I desire?"

To address the issue of preparation for the future, however, we need to first get some understanding of time, without which we have no reference point for anything we do in this life. Secondly, we need to get some understanding of what represents an opportunity. These two essential elements of this book are discussed in the **Getting Started** section following.

This first section entitled **Getting Started** is divided into 5 chapters, namely *"What is Time?"*, *"What is an Opportunity?"*, *"Time and Opportunity – The Winning Combination"*, *"Recognising Opportunities"*, and *"Types of Opportunity"*.

The second section is entitled **"Preparing for Opportunities"**. It consists of 6 chapters, namely *"Are You Preparing for the Future?"*, *"The Reality-Aspiration Check"*, *"Understanding the Need for Change"*, *"Why It Is Not Too Late"*, *"Avoiding Time Wasters"*, and *"Using Time Wisely"*.

The third and final section is entitled **"Going For Opportunities"** and is made up of 5 chapters. These are *"Using Opportunities"*, *"Life is a Giver of Opportunities"*, *"Opportunities and You"*, *"Creating Your Opportunities"* and *"Winning in Life"*.

The book concludes with an invitation or a challenge, depending on how you see it. It is a call to step out and succeed.

Look at commuters on their way to work in the morning or on their way home in the evening. It always seems like a mad rush, whether by car or on trains and buses. Not surprisingly, we call it "the rush hour". But why the rush and where to, if one ever dares to ask themselves or others, that is?

SECTION 1

GETTING STARTED

Looking at those dashing off in their cars or the crowds on the concourses at train or subway stations or those waiting to hop on to buses, one could be deceived into thinking that all these people have a clear picture of where they are going with their lives. On the contrary, most are not living out their dream. That is to say, they are not experiencing the kind of life they had always hoped or dreamed would be their future. Instead, what we see is people going to or coming from an "occupation". Even though we have come to accept the term to mean a job or livelihood, an *occupation* actually refers to something that **takes up our time**.

Mediocrity teaches that such "occupation" is to be desired as the alternative to being idle or unoccupied. Unfortunately, what it does not teach us is the fact that the seemingly better road is not the best road, or to put it bluntly, "average is the enemy of best". Mediocrity leads to the sub-optimal use of our given time leading of course to dissatisfaction.

As Theodore Roosevelt, 26th President of the United States famously said, *"Far better is it to dare mighty things, to win glorious triumphs, even though checkered by failure ... than to rank with those poor spirits who neither enjoy nor suffer much, because they live in a gray twilight that knows not victory nor defeat."*

Chapter 1 introduces the concept of time and why we must optimise its use.

Chapter 2 explains what an opportunity is and also addresses the question of whether there are any opportunities today.

Using time optimally is not just about having an awareness of the value of time, but also the recognition of the presence of a set of factors that must be taken advantage of at a specific point in time, which markedly accelerate our journey towards a desired goal or dream. This is the winning combination for life – *time and opportunity*. This is the subject of **Chapter 3**.

An explanation of how to recognise opportunities then follows in **Chapter 4**.

Chapter 5 concludes the first section of the book by describing the broad categories under which opportunities present themselves.

Chapter 1

What Is Time?

Depending on the specific context in which it is used, time may refer to any of the following:

Space, spell, while, duration, interval, span, stretch, day, epoch, era, period, and season.

According to the Oxford Dictionary, time is "*The indefinite continued progress of existence and events in the past, present, and future regarded as a whole.*"

The Merriam-Webster Dictionary defines time as "*the measured or measurable period during which an action, process, or condition exists or continues*"

Carl Sanburg, who won 3 Pulitzer prizes, said,

"Time is the coin of your life. It is the only coin you have, and only YOU can determine how it will be spent. Be careful lest you let other people spend it for you."

Time in a sense, is a resource that has been made available to each of us. The rich and poor, the successful and unsuccessful, the atheist, agnostic and person of faith, the diligent and the lazy all have 24 hours made available to them every single day. The difference in their conditions or outcomes arises from how this time resource is used or has been used.

Time has also been defined as the passing of life.

Just think about what happens every second, minute, hour or day in our world today?

There are 4 babies delivered with every passing second and at least 100 deaths every minute in the world. The average value of trade on the New York Stock Exchange in a trading hour is $26 billion. In the United Kingdom, over 2,000 new businesses start up every working day.

Time may be seen in context, measured by the number of years, months, weeks, days, hours, minutes and seconds, given to each one of us to complete unique missions. Each person's duration is characterised by its own unique set of objectives or to-do list, distractions, diversions, and unforeseeable events and issues. The goal is to reach the chosen or given target in the given duration, no matter the challenges.

For some unfortunately, nothing gets done. They while away or "kill" time. For others, the sense of urgency makes them run around feverishly, being seen to be busy, but without ever accomplishing much.

Urgency does not mean busyness. Life seems so busy, so full of distractions and "to do" lists. Don't let "busyness" keep you from your real "business", assignment, goal or dream.

Eagerly search for, discover and/or nurture the gifting or talent you have and find ways to make it relevant, using it in service to others. Make a decision to be committed to fulfilling it. Let it be your passion. Use your passion to make that service a key priority in your life each day.

Time is the most perishable commodity in the world

As you read this book, think on the fact that the seconds, minutes and hours that have gone by will never come back. That is why we have to make use of every opportunity – seizing every moment.

The above descriptions give the *"chronos"* definition of time. This is where time is seen as some sequential or a consecutive occurrence of events in a chronological or time-ordered manner. Used in this context, time can be measured quantitatively.

Time may also be understood by its *"kairos"* definition, which refers to a particular moment, a set or appointed time, a season, an opportune situation. In this context, time is indeterminate and is of qualitative nature.

The value of time

The value of time is measured by the kind of decisions and choices a person makes - not the number of decisions and choices - to enable him or her fulfill a role. Time will test the quality of our decisions.

Time is a most precious asset. It is neither renewable nor transferable. It is sad to hear people talk about killing or whiling away time when it is such a scarce and invaluable resource.

Unfortunately, there are many who use most of their productive time on unproductive activities.

Even though the specific value of time may be indeterminate, its value becomes more apparent when we look at its impact.

For instance, ask a student who didn't manage his or her time properly and so fails an exam and has to wait a whole year to re-sit those exams: if only a bit more time had been spent on exam preparation; or ask a mother who delivers a baby one month prematurely: had the baby been delivered at full term, it may not have been exposed to some health risks or challenges; or ask a man who has had a heart attack and is hoping to be resuscitated within minutes: every minute of delayed help or treatment could mean the difference between life and death; or ask a sprint athlete who loses out on the Olympic gold medal by a fraction of a second: if only he or she had gotten out of the starting block fractionally faster.

In each of the above examples, there is a question of timing.

I am reminded of an account given by a survivor of the September 11th 2001 terrorist attack on the twin towers in New York, who said that being caught up in traffic made him get to work late. That lateness due to a traffic jam saved his life. The story teaches a valuable lesson.

Instead of fretting about the snail's pace of movement on life's freeway that is oftentimes accompanied by the road rage that some fall into, we should be grateful and see the bigger picture. This road rage can be likened to the anxiety and impatience that some people exhibit because of some temporary and unpleasant or undesirable circumstances.

As we go about our daily business, we should not lose sight of the bigger picture, which are our goals and aspirations. It will help prioritise our use of time.

Chapter 2

---------- ❋ ----------

What Is An Opportunity?

An opportunity may be defined as *an uncertain event with a positive probable consequence.*

It is also *a favourable or advantageous circumstance or combination of circumstances*

It is often described as *a moment of truth* - a crucial moment on which much depends.

Much talk has been made of opportunities or perhaps the lack of them.

The word "opportunity" comes from the Greek words ***"ob portu"*** connoting the idea of a ship wanting to enter a port, having to wait for the moment when the tide was exactly right to carry it to harbor.

The captain and the crew would wait for the precise moment when the tide is right because they know if they missed it, they would have to wait for another tide to come in.

Thus opportunity refers to a "favourable juncture of circumstances".

William Shakespeare, the great English playwright, used this idea to write one of his famous passages. He said,

> *"There is a tide in the affairs of men, Which,*
> *taken at the flood, leads on to fortune;*
> *Omitted, all the voyage of their life Is*
> *bound in shallows and in miseries. On such*
> *a full sea are we now afloat; And we must*
> *take the current when it serves, Or*
> *lose our venture."*

Opportunities – Are There Really Any?

This is a question that is frequently asked by countless number of people.

Sir Richard Branson, the British entrepreneur who is chairman of the Virgin group, says of opportunities that *"They are like buses, there's always another one coming."*

Ralph Waldo Emerson, an American author, poet and philosopher, said, *"No great man ever complains of want of opportunity."*

Sir Winston Churchill, arguably Britain's best known prime minister and who run the government during the Second World War, says *"A pessimist sees the difficulty in every opportunity; an optimist sees the opportunity in every difficulty."*

Joel Osteen, pastor of Lakewood Church in Houston, Texas, says *"Each of us has pre-arranged opportunities; moments for our future."*

It is clear from these quotes, and also from reading or hearing about the lives of some people, that opportunities still exist.

So if there are opportunities, why are they not being seized by many?

The answer is quite simple: most people do not recognise opportunities easily. The obvious follow-on question would be *"How do we recognise opportunities?"* This will be answered shortly in Chapter 4. In the next chapter, however, we will see how bringing the two concepts together, time and opportunity, can produce a winning combination.

Chapter 3

-------- ❖ --------

Time and Opportunity –
The Winning Combination

Around 835 B.C., King Solomon, the great writer of proverbs, made the following statements:

- **The race is not always for the swift**
- **The strongest does not always win the battle**
- **The wise sometimes go hungry**
- **The skillful are not necessarily wealthy**
- **The educated don't always lead successful lives,**
- **But <u>Time and Opportunity</u> hits us all.**

King Solomon is said to be one of the wisest men that ever lived on earth. The above statements, like many of the other profound statements he made, were born of out his observations and the innate wisdom he possessed.

So what exactly did he mean by these statements?

The following pages illustrate the importance of timing and opportunity.

The Race is not always for the Swift

Have you noticed that it is not always the fastest sprinter that wins a race? Oftentimes the expected winner is nowhere in contention. This could be because the unexpected winner may have gotten off the starting blocks at the right time and therefore gets a head start. This makes it difficult in many cases for the pre-race "favourite" to catch up. Occasionally, some so-called "favourites" get disqualified for false starts or breaking lane rules or are just not ready physically or mentally at the time of the race.

You may think someone or some people have an edge or advantage over you in some way, but life always presents each one of us with a path to reaching greatness and fulfillment.

This reminds me of the story of the tortoise and the hare. The two creatures decided to compete in a race. When the race started, the hare took off with a dash while the tortoise plodded along. However, halfway into the race, the hare decided to take a nap since the competition, the tortoise, was way behind.

Unfortunately, the nap turned into a good sleep from which the hare woke up to find the tortoise almost at the finish point. With all the energy it could muster, the hare raced down the track towards the finishing line in the hope of overtaking the tortoise. Unfortunately, he had left it too late because the slow but steady tortoise won the race.

The story teaches an important lesson in that it is not how one starts out in life that matters, but rather how one finishes. We should never get too comfortable, complacent or overconfident with where we are today otherwise we might be confronted with unpleasant surprises later.

In the space race between the Russians and the Americans, the Russians took the lead in going into space when Yuri Gagarin became the first man into space in 1961. Yet it was an American, Neil Armstrong, who in 1969 became the first man to set foot on the moon.

The Strongest do not always win the Battle

Try to picture two men felling trees in a forest. One of them is a strong well-built man using an axe, and the other is a lean and smallish chap using a chainsaw to bring down a similar sized tree. Which one do you think would be doing more work in trying to cut down the tree?

If you thought the muscular one was doing more work then you were wrong. Yes, he is applying more effort or probably seen as being busier, but it is the lean, smallish person who is doing more work, albeit effortlessly.

Your impact or significance is not measured by how much strength or effort you apply with your undeveloped skills, but rather by the impact and/or effect of applying or using your honed skills.

This explains why a labourer does not usually earn more than a manager in the same work place. It is about the size of the problem being solved, not the size of the effort being applied.

When boxing legend, Muhammad Ali, had the historic world heavyweight title bout with George Foreman in Kinshasa, Congo, in 1974, it was not George's powerful punch that determined the outcome of the bout, but rather the maneuvering skills displayed by Ali.

The Wise sometimes go Hungry

Sometimes, in a time of plenty or comfort, we forget to prepare for a dry day. Even some insects make better decisions than many humans often do.

Ants may be little creatures, but they prepare in advance for any eventuality. Perhaps we can learn a lesson from them about preparing for our future, so that that we are properly positioned to capitalise on opportunities.

We can also learn from conies, which may be feeble creatures, but yet they make daring moves that seem inconceivable for their size.

Locusts are often perceived as destructive creatures by many because of the havoc they cause to crops. But what is fascinating about them is that despite having no leader, they can move in bands over hundreds of miles. Synergy through working together can enable us accomplish much more than we could ever have dreamed of.

The Skillful are not necessarily Wealthy

The story is told of a poor wise man whose advice helped to deliver a city under siege. Yet no one remembered him afterwards because wisdom that does not translate into personal success is not usually taken seriously.

In life, it is not what you do for a profession or pursue as a career that makes you successful, but rather the manner and place where you use your skills.

There are poor and wealthy people in every profession on earth. What distinguishes the latter is their ability to harness their resources and convert them into opportunities.

To illustrate the point, if people were asked only a few years ago whom they thought was the most skillful soccer player in the world at the time, most people knowledgeable about the sport would mention names other than that of David Beckham. So why was he among the best paid soccer players in the world? Unlike his contemporaries, David found a way to price his skills as part of a package that made many top soccer club managers want to have him as part of their team.

The Educated don't always lead Successful Lives

There has always been a perception, albeit a wrong one, that acquiring an education brings success. If that were the case, the most successful people on earth would be university professors.

I have found that it is not what a person studies as a discipline that necessarily makes a difference in life, but rather the quality of the decisions and actions taken by the person. These can have positive or negative consequences.

The decisions and actions that lead to success include wise planning, common sense, getting abreast with the necessary facts, and taking bold steps. Decisions decide wealth.

Chapter 4

------- ❖ -------

Recognising Opportunities

Thomas Edison, who developed the electric light bulb, said, *"An opportunity is missed by most because it is dressed in overalls and looks like work."*

Albert Einstein, the famous physicist who developed the theory of relativity, said, *"In the middle of every difficulty lies opportunity."*

As Charles R. Swindoll, an American writer and clergyman said, *"We are all faced with a series of great opportunities brilliantly disguised as impossible situations."*

Unless an opportunity is expected or prepared for, a given one may not be recognised early, if at all.

A person's perception or outlook may therefore positively or negatively affect his or her ability to recognise a given opportunity or one that is in the making.

Take for instance, a person who sees financial gifts or support as the only means of making progress with their lives or on a specific project. An offer of work, whether paid or voluntary, will be spurned when in fact it could be providing the means to become self-sufficient or less dependent.

Another scenario is that of a skilled person who has been out of work for some time and is getting increasingly frustrated at the inability to find suitable employment. As earning a salary is the only perceived way of getting money, starting up on his or her own or with someone else does not cross the mind or seems inconceivable.

Another important note about opportunities is that they do not always come as some great big door open for us. Some opportunities do not look very obvious as they come as *windows of opportunity* or *slivers of opportunity*.

Chapter 5

Types of Opportunity

Windows of Opportunity

A window of opportunity provides a short period of time during which an opportunity must be acted on or missed.

Life does provide us with windows of opportunity, which when seized, will gradually lead us to the realisation of our desired goals.

One such story is that of Alfredo Quinones-Hinojosa.

In the late 1980s, Alfredo got into the United States from Mexico in the hope of bettering his life. But unlike many others before him and after him, he had a sense of mission.

He started by picking weeds, and then got a better job working a tractor. He then moved on to become a welder. He was later able to go to a community college and learnt English, followed later by studies at the University of California, Berkeley. He then got his U.S. citizenship and a scholarship to Harvard Medical School, where he graduated *cum laude*.

Alfredo became a Professor of Neurosurgery and Oncology, Neuroscience and Cellular and Molecular Medicine at Johns Hopkins University and also served as the Director of its Brain Tumour Surgery Program.

Today, Alfredo is Professor and Chair of Neurologic Surgery at the Mayo Clinic in Jacksonville, Florida.

Alfredo achieved his dream, not through a big door opening to him, but through a series of small or intermediate steps.

In January 1954, a baby girl was born out of wedlock to a teenage housemaid in Kosciusko, Mississippi in the United States. She was raised by her grandmother for her first few years. Suffering abuse and rape when she moved to her mother's place in Milwaukee for the second time, she run away and eventually moved to Nashville, Tennessee to live with her father.

With his oversight, she took her studies seriously, and graduated from high school. She later graduated from Tennessee State University and then went on to become a TV news anchor. Through a succession of other roles with different networks and stations, she eventually started running her own talk show.

Today, Oprah Winfrey, the African-American media mogul, talk show host, actress, producer, and philanthropist is impacting lives in different parts of the world.

Slivers of Opportunity

A sliver of opportunity is like a tiny or small opening in a door just big enough to put a foot through; once the first step is taken, it could lead to other opportunities coming up, and the door opening wider. Unlike a window of opportunity, a sliver of opportunity may not have limited time duration, and so may remain open for a while.

Take for instance, someone who has been looking for an analyst job in some discipline for a long time without success and is still unemployed. Yet during that same period of waiting, there has been another job opportunity beckoning even though it may not be as glamorous as the desired job but still falls within the same general area of work. This job opening presents a sliver that could be utilised – a given opportunity to get into a firm, industry or to network with those in the desired area.

Doors of Opportunity

A door of opportunity is like a dream come true. It is a favourable set of circumstances that beckons to someone. Doors of opportunity can present themselves at any time. For the person who has adequately prepared for the opportunity, it is truly golden.

Alexander Graham Bell, who invented the telephone, said, *"When one door closes, another opens; but often we look so long and so regretfully at the closed door that we do not see the one which has been opened for us."*

Lakhsmi Mittal, a steel magnate and one of Britain's richest men, said, *"Always think outside the box and embrace opportunities that appear, wherever they might be."*

Debasish Mridha, an American physician, writer and philosopher said, *"The more I learn, the more doors of information and opportunity are open to me."*

Chris Widener, a personal development and leadership expert, wrote, *"Those who succeed are those who walk through the door of opportunity when it swings open. That we know. But what is the secret to getting through the door of opportunity? [It's] Being outside the door when it swings open."*

Despite the many opportunities life may present to us, there are those times when there appear to be none. The difference between those who succeed in reaching their goals and those who do not, is often the level of preparedness of the former and also their ability to create opportunities while the latter wring their hands in frustration or take a mediocre path.

SECTION 2

PREPARING FOR OPPORTUNITIES

Good preparation usually leads to good performance. This section looks specifically at what is required to ensure you are well prepared for opportunities. Chapter 6 looks specifically at the question, "*Are You Preparing for the Future?*"

Embarking on a journey into your future, as with every journey, requires deciding on a destination and defining a starting point. This is where what I term a *Reality-Aspiration Check* is helpful. This personal or organisational exercise is detailed in Chapter 7.

The purpose of the Reality-Aspiration Check is to bring you to a place of decision. It will enable you to see what your shortcomings and/or what the challenges are in relation to the realisation of your dreams.

This recognition is important in deciding an appropriate course of action. As an individual, this would mean devising a detailed plan to move you from your current situation and get you to a desired goal. As an organisation, it will help to craft a strategy to achieve or sustain competitive advantage.

There are some for whom moving from the plan to experiencing a dream requires breaking free from the fear of commitment. A fear of commitment to carry through whatever decisions are made can hold you back because it is only in committing yourself to a course of action that you make progress with your life, making the most of the opportunities that come your way.

Whether for a simple or an elaborate plan of action, the same mental processes are involved. This is why we need to **change our mindset, attitude, perception and expectation** from one of pessimism or indifference, to one of optimism. Chapter 8 highlights the importance of "*Understanding the Need for Change*".

Reminiscing on a life of regret or projecting a future of gloom will only exacerbate your present condition. The current situation is not permanent. It is not too late to create a better future. This is the reassuring news that Chapter 9 brings under the heading "*Why it is Not Too Late*".

Your actions today will determine the kind of future you create for yourself. This means doing away with time-wasting activities and avoiding or minimising contact with those who sap your productive time. Time-wasting activities are those tasks and engagements that do not add value to your life. Chapter 10 elaborates on this under the theme "*Avoiding Time Wasters*".

With each passing day, make wise choices, including your use of time. Paul, the great New Testament writer, puts it succinctly when he writes:

- **Redeem the time because we live in dangerous times;**
- **Don't be foolish, but rather understand what is paramount;**
- **Make the most of every opportunity.**

Creating free or spare time by avoiding time-wasting activities may be good, but not enough to guarantee fruitfulness or productivity. As has been said, "Idle hands are the devil's workshop". It is important to make the best use of the given time. That's why this second section of the book ends with Chapter 11 on "*Using Time Wisely*".

Chapter 6

---------- ❖ ----------

Are You Preparing for the Future?

Putting the Past behind You

Don't get stuck in the past – its successes or failures, its savoury moments or the disappointments experienced.

Have you heard people reminisce about something good, exciting or positive in their past? If so, you might have heard the phrase "good old days". Perhaps you have been using that phrase yourself. Yes, there may have been some good times, but we need to remember that yesterday is in the grave.

Even though starting a journey on the right note is good, it is more important to complete the journey, and to complete it properly. This means our future is more important than our past.

One can find numerous stories of individuals born with a silver spoon in their mouth or born into royalty who ended up in a despicable state. We also find organisations that were the pace-setters and/or market leaders in their heydays that have lost their glory. Conversely, we read of people or organisations that started poorly and yet have achieved remarkable success today.

So don't spend the time gloating over past "successes" or brooding over past "failures". Each passing moment presents us with an opportunity to either correct or improve our lot from yesterday.

Neither should you be glued to the present because today's extraordinary achievements may become commonplace or mundane tomorrow.

History is fraught with examples of individuals, some of whom you may be personally acquainted with, who accomplished what was considered unimaginable feats only a short while ago. Today, their influence has clearly diminished. In the case of organisations, they may no longer be in operation.

Take, for example, the agility of Jamaican sprinter, Asafa Powell, who astounded his rivals and spectators with his superb performances in 100-metre races. Just as pundits were getting used to the idea of him being the race "favourite", fellow countryman, Usain Bolt, took the world by storm. Usain immediately drowned out the competition, and like his surname suggests, with lightning bolt speed.

This is why you need to prepare for the future.

The purpose of this book is to stir you to create a future for yourself, your loved ones, your organisation – a bright future or even brighter future than you are currently expecting.

This book carries a fundamental theme:

No matter your age or circumstances,
As long as you have life,
There is always <u>Time and Opportunity</u>.

Chapter 7

The Reality-Aspiration Check

This is a self-enquiry process meant to determine what it would take to reach a desired destination. It involves asking and honestly answering four simple questions.

As Chinese philosopher, Lao Tzu, said, ***"Knowing others is wisdom, knowing yourself is enlightenment."***

1st Question – Where Are You Today?

This has to do with your present circumstances or situation. Your circumstance is where you're at as at today.

The Free Dictionary defines a circumstance as *"A condition or fact that determines or must be considered in the determining of a course of action."*

Are you …..

- **Unemployed and/or have you given up trying to get employed or be self-employed?**
- **A self-financing student trying to juggle competing pressures and possibly work restrictions due to academic schedule, family, legal or other constraint?**
- **A recent graduate who has moved or is moving from euphoria and high expectations, an atmosphere which college graduation ceremonies seem to create, to a place of uncertainty and disappointment as time has elapsed?**
- **An unhappy employee who has had enough of the work environment?**
- **Overwhelmed with indebtedness, insolvency or other financial challenges?**
- **Battling with illness?**
- **Facing marital or other relational challenges?**
- **Struggling to meet your obligations or to maintain your operations as a business?**

- **Disillusioned or frustrated with your current state of affairs?**

Perhaps, unlike most people, you are satisfied – with a great job, a wonderful family, or part of an organisation that seems to be doing well or better than average. Even at that, there is always more to accomplish, not necessarily for you, but for the benefit of others.

For many, the object of living has become mere survival, a treadmill exercise really; progress, at best, has been at a snail's pace; steam has been taken out of their initial burst of energy and exuberance; daily pressures and constant challenges seem to have taken their toll, giving them an outlook of despair and a perpetuity of mediocre existence, or in extreme cases, an anticipation of evil foreboding, except for some miraculous intervention. This is also true for many organisations.

This reality is a far cry from their hopes and dreams, which seem to have dissipated altogether.

Taking cognisance of where you are today leads to asking the next question:

2nd Question – What Is Your Ultimate Aspiration?

An aspiration is a will to succeed, a cherished desire, a longing ambition, an objective desire.

What do you want to be in the future? As an individual, is it to be a key political figure, a fantastic home-maker, a superb manager, a successful business person, a notable educator, an influential community leader, an inventor, a great entertainer or legendary sportsperson? As a start-up, is it to be a thriving business or do more community impacting? As a thriving business, is it to be the market leader in your industry or region?

What picture do you have of yourself for the future? Some would call this a dream or vision. A vision is a picture of your desired future. I am reminded of the proverb, which says that without a clear vision, a person walks aimlessly and lives carelessly.

Are you living one day at a time without a sense of mission or clear strategy or are you steadily working daily towards your goals?

Across the globe, many carry on with their lives without a clearly-defined purpose, only to realise regretfully much later that they have not accomplished anything meaningful.

Sadly, you will find people who work all their lives doing what they do not enjoy and then retire to then begin to do what they had always enjoyed but never gave time to. Their working lives ran like a treadmill, characterised by drudgery and self-inflicted confinement. The only accolade attesting to their decades of hard work is a certificate of appreciation for the tenure of long service, sometimes accompanied by a wall clock or other ceremonial gesture of appreciation from an employer. Without sounding cynical, the ticking of the wall clock might serve as a reminder of the brevity of time to "make up" for the lost time.

Some reading this book may say "That will never happen to me." Unfortunately, unless appropriate steps are taken, this undesirable outcome could be repeated for many.

Life is not a joke. It is not a movie-on-demand that one can pause, rewind or replay at will. For each one of us, we have only one run. How we run our chosen or given course will determine the kind of rewards we receive at the end.

Since your career or job is something that occupies a large part of your day or possibly even your life, why not do something that you enjoy doing? Have fun doing what you do, and earn money while doing so.

A professor friend of mine once joked about his consulting work and seminars that have taken him to numerous countries around the world, saying "I like to travel business class at other people's expense."

In 2006, I saw an interesting job advert in a local newspaper in London. A hotel chain was looking to recruit a Sleep Consultant. Yes, you read right – a Sleep Consultant. The position required testing the quality of beds for the hotel's guests by sleeping on them. If the consultant did not enjoy sleeping on any bed, it meant that bed was below standard. For the "hard" work, the successful applicant would earn $100,000 a year!

Have a desire to achieve something – something noble, something great. Don't set your sights on something mediocre. It is much better to attempt something great and fail than not to make any attempt at all. Focus on achieving something that you are passionate about – something that will benefit others, even if not all of humanity.

Remember, your vision is your future, and no dream is too big.

3rd Question – What is Your Greatest Fear?

Fear is that which causes a feeling of being afraid. It is apprehension, fright, anxiety, and agitation.

It is a distressing emotion aroused by impending danger, evil and pain – whether the threat is real or imagined.

There is a kind of fear that is acceptable. It is a kind of restraining condition that keeps us from losing our integrity or reputation or from falling on the wrong side of the law. For instance, the fear of getting caught doing something illegal such as trafficking or perhaps a fear of the taxman. This is not the kind of fear being talked about here.

Many have a vision of what they want to be in the future but instead of focusing on the big picture, they train their eyes on the obstacles, difficulties or problems they may encounter. Sometimes, these negatives are imaginary.

Are you afraid of failure – failing your exams, losing your job, your business collapsing, or a relationship breaking down?

Are you scared of money-related problems – such as indebtedness, bankruptcy or losing a property through foreclosure or falling into abject poverty?

Or perhaps you are afraid of committing to a long-term relationship like marriage or losing your independence. Are you afraid of infertility, pregnancy, child birth or parenting?

Are you afraid of violence such as terrorism, rape or gangs?

Maybe it is some other phobia – of heights, of the dark, of the future.

Are you afraid of growing old or of dying – without fulfilling your dream?

I recall a conversation I had with an international participant a couple of years ago who was attending a training course I was delivering in London. It happened to be her first visit to London and she wanted to do some shopping in Central London, so I asked her to use the subway instead of the buses to save her time, but her response was that she was not comfortable with travelling on the trains, as there had been a bombing in London involving trains 2 years earlier.

Fear is a dangerous thing. It inhibits creativity, stops the taking of positive action and limits progress. As has been said, "The only thing to fear is fear itself". Fear is like a force that attracts. The more a fear is dwelt on, thought about or meditated on, the larger it looms.

It has been said that the difference between a brave person and a coward is that the brave one does not outwardly show that they are afraid.

4th Question – What is Your Biggest Challenge?

A challenge is different from a fear. A challenge is a call to fight, a contest of skill or strength. It is to dare or question

.

You might be saying:

- **I have no one to help me financially;**
- **I have a poor education;**
- **I have work restrictions or career limitations;**
- **I have poor communication skills;**
- **I have a disability or am physically challenged;**
- **I face gender biases or other prejudice;**
- **I lack self-confidence.**

Each of the above reasons may indicate a seemingly insurmountable situation or issue. The truth is that all the above reasons are not big enough to stop a person from realising their dreams.

A challenge is a situation that must be overcome in order to ensure that something we are afraid of does not materialise. It calls for confronting an issue.
Identifying what the challenges are is a necessary step for developing winning solutions.

For many years, I had a fear of heights. Merely standing near the window of some high rise building would send shivers down my spine. In February 2005, while undertaking a project in St. Vincent and the Grenadines, a beautiful island state in the Caribbean, I was invited to join a mountain climbing expedition. Naturally, I gave myself all the reasons why I could not accept the invitation, but on the morning of the event, I told myself that I needed to confront my fear and that the expedition presented me with an opportunity to do just that. I am glad I accomplished that feat.

See the challenge as a summit to reach and not as a mountain to climb.

Challenges present us with the opportunity to muster our given resources, both internal and external, to address something confronting us. Those able to accomplish this find more bounce in their steps, have greater tenacity and a stronger resolve to beat all odds and excel.

To borrow a quote from Marilyn Allen, an American motivational speaker, educator and social worker, **"If the DREAM is BIG Enough, the Facts Don't Matter."**

"I have answered the four questions. So what's next?" you might ask.

Without oversimplifying the process, the following are essential steps *(it might be worth having a small notebook handy or a tablet as you go through this exercise to enable you put your thoughts, reflections, decisions, and planned actions on paper)*:

1. Take a little time to get a proper understanding of what the Reality-Aspiration Check produced, that is, its implications for you at the present time. Read through it several times, if you must.

2. Ask yourself what key decisions you need to make. It is important that you have a clear understanding of what it is you need to do. For an organisation, you might call this the critical success factors.

3. Begin to identify viable options based on your interests, skills, values, and personality characteristics. Your options may not necessarily be in one particular area. For instance, someone may focus only on the professional area. Another person may focus on family/relationships and also health or business.

4. Gather and examine the information and other resources you currently have and determine what is missing. Fill in the gaps as best as you can, including getting help from others. The internet offers a plethora of resources. Some might solicit the help of coaches and mentors.

5. Evaluate your options, including resources needed, risks involved, and consequences of choosing each option.

6. Select one of the alternatives.

7. Prepare an action plan to implement the selected alternative. What is required to complete each step? What are the obstacles to completing the steps? How should these obstacles be overcome?

At the end of this exercise you will have a game plan to move you in the direction of your goals.

The above steps, even though essential, will give only limited success unless you recognise the need for certain changes (if they haven't already taken place). These changes have to do with YOU.

Chapter 8

Understanding the Need for Change

In answering the four preceding questions, you probably identified with some of the examples given. For some of you, it may have been an opportunity to do some soul-searching or quiet reflection.

This may have left you perplexed at your inability to do something about your situation, or feeling angry at yourself for not taking action sooner, or frustrated in not being sure what to do next, or perhaps resigning yourself in self-pity.

Whatever your reaction, what is important is to recognise that it is time for a change.

There are four key things to change, and the time to do that is NOW. These are *your mindset, your attitude, your perception or outlook, and your expectation.* Putting off any necessary changes will delay or prevent the realisation of your life goals.

Mindset

A mindset is a set of beliefs or a way of thinking held by one or more persons or groups of people that determines behaviour, outlook or mental attitude.

It creates a powerful incentive within these people or groups to continue to adopt or accept prior behaviours, choices, or methods.

The following mindsets have been used to describe human tendencies: *the mouse mindset, chicken mindset, donkey mindset, crow mindset, peacock mindset and an eagle mindset.*

The **mouse mindset** is characterised by timidity and following the same routine in spite of undesirable outcomes in the past, whether from a person's own experience or those of others.

It reminds me of a funny quote I came across several years ago at an insurance education institute in The Gambia that I had done some work for. The quote was attributed to one of the institute's professors. It said

"A fool is always a fool, even when he has gone to school."

In other words, education really wouldn't make a difference to someone who was stuck in a particular mode of thinking.

Unfortunately, this tendency is exhibited by many in different parts of the world. An example is a person being educated to a doctorate level say in political science and yet when it comes to voting for someone for political office this "educated" person chooses to vote on ethnic or party lines without giving any credence to the manifesto of the candidate or those of the candidate's rivals.

The mouse mentality is also exhibited when a boy is schooled by his parents to study hard and go to college so that he can get a good civil service job and security for life. The boy indeed graduates from college, gets a civil service job, later becomes a parent and now gives his children the same advice even though he has experienced the stresses and disappointments the job has brought him. The issue is not about going to college and/or getting a civil service job, but rather the fact that he has never given thought to any other option. In other words, caught up in an 8-to-4 or 9-to-5 work mentality.

The mouse mentality leaves no room for experimentation and is not open to new ideas. It reminds me of the proverbial quote by Nigerian novelist, poet, and critic, Chinua Achebe in his book, Things Fall Apart. It said, *"Eneke the bird says that since men have learned to shoot without missing, he has learned to fly without perching."* Even the bird got smarter and started doing things differently.

The **chicken mindset** is characterised by short-sightedness, lack of stamina, aimlessness, passivity, and easy-going or settler thinking. This mindset reflects those who live in the "comfort zone".

An example is a person who has recognised the need to leave an unsatisfactory job but is afraid to do so because it could result in losing the sense of security derived from the job.

This mindset reflects the position of those who are fearful of the unknown and therefore always prefer the cautious, mediocre approach. They never want to venture out for fear of something.

Victor Kwegyir, business coach and consultant, describes them as *"Creating all sorts of mountains and obstacles in their head."*

In a relational context, people with this mindset settle for marriages of convenience - platonic at best but struggling at their core in most cases.

As Norva Semoy Abiona, relationship expert, life coach and businesswoman points out, they always have a ready excuse for their inaction.

The **donkey mindset** is characterised by low self-esteem and negative thinking. This may be the case of people who have gone through some kind of trauma, rejection or have been abused in one way or other. They dwell on their past experience and have no positive expectations.

The donkey attribution is because it takes a boot, a kick, to get them moving. It sometimes take a crisis to bring an awakening to them.

As John Maxwell, American leadership expert, speaker and author said, *"Once our minds are 'tattooed' with negative thinking, our chances for long-term success diminish."*

The **crow mindset** is characterised by noise (noticeably loud, but not making a positive impact), boastful and by being argumentative or defensive, critical or distracting. Like Kin Hubbard, an American cartoonist, humourist, and journalist, said, *"Some* *folks can look so busy doing nothing that they seem indispensable."*

People exhibiting this mindset were described by a 19th century British Prime Minister and novelist, Benjamin Disraeli, as finding it *"easier to be critical than correct."*

The crow mindset often characterises people who want to get involved in everything and/or want to pull others into whatever they are involved in.

The crow mindset gives a false sense of security to those that have it. It carries a false notion that being busy equates to being productive. It usually is not open to correction or reasoning.

The **peacock mindset** is exhibited by those who are self-centred and self-obsessed. They like being at the centre of attention and they crave the balm of constant praise and reassurance. They are egotistic.

The issue for those with this mindset is that they find collaboration and teamwork difficult. They may be star performers in their own right but can't stand or don't enjoy not being in the limelight. They love being accredited with any semblance of success. They often fail to realise that teamworking creates synergy and makes greater impact. Their lone wolf preference means they often miss out on many great opportunities.

Sometimes the peacock mindset reflects a false projection of success or of 'having it all together' when in reality there are issues being battled with behind the façade.

As Pope Francis of Assisi said, *"look at the peacock; it's beautiful if you look at it from the front. But if you look at it from behind, you discover the truth ..."*

The **eagle mindset** characterises those with a clear vision, the ability to weather storms, being focused, dogged, resolute, proactive, and being a fighter or an overcomer. As Charles R. Swindoll said, *"People who soar are those who refuse to sit back and wish things would change."*

Mike Murdock, of the Wisdom Center in Dallas, Texas puts it this way: *"Intolerance of your present schedules your future."*

The eagle mindset is essential for winning in life. Life does not often give us the luxury of choosing what comes against us. It is therefore essential to be able to weather its storms and to come out on top. I like the truth statement that says *"He who cannot stand the test of adversity is made of inferior material."*

Attitude

An attitude is defined as the manner, disposition, feeling or position, with regard to a person or thing; it is a tendency or orientation, especially of the mind.

Your attitudes are the established ways of responding to people and situations that you have learned, based on the beliefs, values and assumptions you hold.

Your attitude will determine your altitude. Your attitude is the key determinant in whether you succeed or you fail. A negative or defeatist attitude will hinder your progress in life.

Abraham Lincoln, who became the 16th president of the United States after a series of unsuccessful runs for political office at different stages in his life, said, *"Always bear in mind that your own resolution to succeed is more important than any other one thing."*

M. Scott Peck, an American psychiatrist and author, says *"The truth is that our finest moments are most likely to occur when we are feeling deeply uncomfortable, unhappy, or unfulfilled. For it is only in such moments, propelled by our discomfort, that we are likely to step out of our ruts and start searching for different ways or truer answers."*

Your attitude determines your approach to life. This is why you need a positive and right attitude towards your life and the future.

Perspective

A perspective is the choice of a context for opinions, beliefs and experiences.

What do you see in other people?

Harold Nicolson, a Persian-born English writer and author said, *"We are all inclined to judge ourselves by our ideals; others, by their acts."*

What do you see in situations?

Irish playwright, George Bernard Shaw said, *"Some look at things that are, and ask why. I dream of things that never were and ask why not?"*

What do you see in yourself?

Dr Mike Murdock says *"Your Self-Portrait Determines What You Are Willing To Endure.*

Your Self-Portrait Will Create An Environment That Supports It."

When you look at yourself do you see a winner or loser, a giant or midget, a voiceless and/or passive spectator of life or an active difference maker? The right perspective is important because *"What you see is what you get."*

What you can't perceive, you can't conceive.

What you can't conceive, you can't receive.

Is the obstacle you may be currently facing a stumbling block or a stepping stone? Is it time to quit or time to be bold and creative?

Expectation

An expectation is the degree of probability that something will occur.

It differs from an aspiration in that, while an aspiration asks the question "How far would you like to go in life?" an expectation asks *"How far do you think you will actually go in life?"*

Sam Walton, American businessman and entrepreneur who founded Wal-Mart, said, *"High expectations are the key to everything."*

Author and motivator, Ralph Marston, says *"Don't lower your expectations to meet your performance. Raise your level of performance to meet your expectations. Expect the best of yourself, and then do what is necessary to make it a reality."*

As a person, I have learnt to set higher standards for myself than people expect of me. This is because other people's expectation of you is often based on what they see - who you are now and what you currently have - as opposed to your potential and your capability.

Thomas Edison said, *"If we did the things we are capable of, we would astound ourselves."*

Finally, it is important to add that **having a tenacious faith or belief is essential for accomplishing the extraordinary**.

The best news of all for each of us is the fact that it is not too late, even now, to change our mindset, attitude, outlook, and expectations.

Simply put, it is not too late to fulfill your dreams.

Chapter 9

Why It Is Not Too Late

It is not too late to change the current situation.

For many, it sometimes appears like it's all over. They see their lives ebbing away. They don't see a way out of their current myriad of problems or a way into something more dignifying, more rewarding or more fulfilling.

Very often, problems or challenges appear bigger than they actually are. This is where a person's perspective becomes important. It requires looking at the bigger picture. To do this, one has to take a step back to see the situation in context. Does it change the fact that there is a problem or challenge? No, it does not.

The difference however is that, when a person does not look at the bigger picture, panic sets in. Those who look at the bigger picture recognise the fact that there is sense of urgency, but do not panic. The latter category are more likely to take the appropriate steps to address any problems or overcome challenges than those who hit the panic button.

Several years ago, I attended an open day event on the campus of a reputable UK university, together with some students from a private college. As we left the campus later that afternoon, I asked a couple of them if they would like to attend that university. A young lady gave me an emphatic "Yes", but then quickly added "but not in my wildest dreams, as I can't afford the high fees".

That led to my asking a few questions about her work plan and income level at the time. As I broke down the annual university fees into monthly and then weekly amounts, it suddenly dawned on her that she only needed to make a little more money each week after some minor changes in her spending habits to be able to afford the "high" fees. Instead of allowing panic to suspend her reasoning, I got her to see the big picture, from which she could craft a strategy for winning. She ended up attending another university better suited to her career that charges fees that she would have hitherto considered exorbitant and out of reach.

The pages following immediately tell the stories of ordinary people like you and me, who refused to make excuses. These are people who refused to accept other people's opinion of their situation. These are accounts of people, some of whom found themselves in situations that would make whatever you may be facing minuscule by comparison.

For these, and countless others whose stories are not narrated here, failure was not an option; "average" was not in their vocabulary; and "it's too late" was not a card on their table.

Some years ago, I was invited to an event at the Los Angeles Convention Center to mark the tenth anniversary of the State of the Black Union. As I listened to distinguished and erudite persons speak in turn about their community specifically and also about the United States in general, I found their personal stories enchanting. They looked like ordinary people and indeed in appearance they were. However, a stark difference became evident as they each spoke. They came from the same communities as millions of others and probably had experienced the same prejudices, but their vision, declarations and outcomes were markedly different. These were clearly men and women who were relentless in their efforts to see better days, not for themselves as they were already accomplished people, but for the communities they came from and also for future generations.

A famous quote from motivational speaker, Les Brown, who was one of the speakers at the event, probably says it best: *"It's not over until you win."*

It is not too late to GET AN EDUCATION

"The illiterate of the 21st century will not be those who cannot read and write, but those who cannot learn, unlearn, and relearn."
Alvin Toffler - American writer and futurist

Kimani Ng'ang'a Maruge (from Kenya) had always dreamed of going to school, but never got that opportunity until 2004, when free education became available in his hometown district.

At 84 years, Kimani started primary school!! "You are never too old to learn," said Kimani. "At no time ever say, 'It's too late to learn,' not until the day you die."

In September 2005, Kimani was invited to New York to address the United Nations Millennium Development Summit. Speaking through an interpreter (having been in school for only one year), he advocated for free primary education for all. What an opportunity, and how selfless his demeanor!!

Despite his frailty, Kimani was looking forward not only to complete his primary and high school education, but to also complete a veterinary diploma and to a brighter future. He died in August 2009, leaving an indelible mark on many excuse-makers.

In July 2008, 91-year-old former soldier, Michael Cobb, became one of the oldest people to receive a doctorate from Cambridge University.
The World War II veteran earned his PhD by creating an atlas of railway stations built in Britain between 1807 and 1994.

In 2012, Bertie (Bert) Gladwin graduated from the University of Buckingham with a Master of Arts degree in Military Intelligence. He was 90 years old.

Bert, a British World War II veteran, had also acquired his 2 bachelors' degrees after his retirement from his British Secret Service career, having left school at the age of 14 in 1935.

Asked if he would recommend a return to formal education after retirement, his answer was an emphatic "YES".

He said, *"You are never too old to learn; it's a pleasure to be able to carry on learning through your life and makes the experience all the more enjoyable."*

Akasease Kofi Boakye Yiadom, from Ghana, graduated from a three-year degree programme in 2010 at the age of 99. The World War II veteran said, *"Education has no end. As far as your brain can work all right, your eyes can see all right and your ears can hear all right, if you go to school you can learn."*

As American author, Brian Herbert said, *"The capacity to learn is a gift; The ability to learn is a skill; The willingness to learn is a choice."*

Perhaps you dropped out of school early due to family or financial reasons or your own poor choices. Or you did complete college but have not studied or done anything more since. *"So what do I need to do, or how do I start?"* you might ask.

Even if you have been out of formal schooling for decades, it does not preclude you from expanding your knowledge base.

Amy Craton first enrolled for a bachelor's degree in 1962, but then left college to raise her four children. She returned in 2013, more than 50 years later, and graduated in 2016 with a 4.0 GPA.

The 94-year-old who lives in Hawaii earned her degree in Creative Writing and English via Southern New Hampshire University online programme. She says, ***"It feels good to graduate, but in many ways I feel I am still on the road; I have more to learn."*** She has since enrolled on an MA degree programme.

Make use of educational and personal development opportunities and avenues. It does not have to be formal education like attending a college.

Like business philosopher, Jim Rohn, said, ***"Formal education will make you a living; self-education will make you a fortune."***

There are other sources like the internet, TV, radio, seminars, as well as a vast array of educational resources on digital media including CDs and DVDs.

On the internet, there are loads of free and paid resources including live streaming conferences and webinars, on-demand videos on YouTube, online education outlets including free university lecture sessions and materials, podcasts and online communities.

Have an enquiring mind. If you have children or grandchildren, teach them the same. One of my key interests is the airline industry, so whenever I come across information relating to that – whether it's about new commercial aircraft, airports, airline management, routing, disasters, etc – I try and get as much information as possible. You will be amazed at the wealth of information you will have amassed in a short space of time.

Develop a reading culture. Cultivate your mind by developing a habit of reading. A reading culture reduces time that a person could have been idle, filling that time with reading useful material. Read biographies, success stories, and other literature that stretch your thinking and strengthen your belief. If you are a slow reader, register on a training programme that teaches speed reading. If you find reading difficult, then listen to audio material and/or watch educative videos.

Find a mentor. Dr Mike Murdock puts it aptly when he says *"There are two ways to increase wisdom: mistakes and mentors." "Mentorship is wisdom without the pain"*, he adds. There is always someone who not only has the knowledge but also can do something you desire to do better than you can at the present time. Learn from such a person, even if they are younger than you. Mentors are not to be seen as your friends. These are people who give you some level of access to the resource you desire. This access should be respected and protected.

It is neither too early nor too late to FIND PURPOSE

It might be pretty obvious that it may not be too late to find and achieve your mandate on our planet. However, most people do not realise that it is never too early to find their purpose in life.

Bilaal Rajan (born September 7, 1996 in Toronto, Canada) is a fundraiser, motivational speaker, author, United Nations Children's Fund (UNICEF) Canada's child ambassador, and founder of the Hands for Help organisation.

Rajan began fundraising when he was four years old, selling clementines door-to-door in his neighborhood to raise C$350 in funds for the *victims of the earthquakes in the Gujarat province of India in 2001.*

He has raised several million dollars for various causes, and in March 2005 he was chosen as an official ambassador for UNICEF.

In 2008, he published "Making Change: Tips from an Underage Overachiever", which focuses on how young people can work together in their local communities to increase awareness about global issues and raise funds for those in need.

He is currently studying at Stanford University.

Malala Yousifazi, born July 12th 1997, is a Pakistani activist for female education and the youngest Nobel Prize laureate. She started blogging for the BBC at an early age. She is known for human rights advocacy, where her work has grown into an international movement particularly when her story broke across the world in 2012. She has only recently started her studies at Oxford University.

Nelson Mandela became President in South Africa in 1994, four years after being released from prison. He did not let 27 years of being in prison stop him from making history. What kept him sane? How did he keep his focus? How did he pick up or hold on to his dream?

Perhaps you or someone close to you may have been in and now out of prison and wondering if life has anything positive to offer. Even where the criminal justice system appears flawed or sometimes discriminatory, that should not preclude anyone from a better future.

Again your perception will determine how far you can go. Do you see a life of banishment because of your possible exclusion from government support or work? Or do you see an opportunity to pick up any pieces, build your life from the opportunities you recognise, which others without your experience do not?

Have you thought about how others, ex-convicts and inmates alike, will be positively impacted by your success story?

Like Nelson Mandela said, *"It always seems impossible, until it's done."* and *"There is no passion to be found playing small - in settling for a life that is less than the one you are capable of living."*

Kellie Lim was eight years old when a raging infection of bacterial meningitis forced the amputation of both legs below the knee, her right hand and forearm, and three fingertips on her left hand.

Eighteen years later, she graduated from UCLA Medical School in California, defying all odds and handicaps. She went on to do her residency in pediatrics.

Kellie said it was inspiration, determination, hard work and the fact that she made no excuses that made the difference.

Kellie went on to pursue fellowship training in allergy and immunology and pharmacology.

Today, she works as an allergist-immunologist at the UCLA Medical Center.

It is not too late to ACQUIRE NEW SKILLS

A change of focus or direction is sometimes all one needs to become successful or even more successful.

George Foreman has retired twice from boxing. In 1994, at the age of 46, he became the oldest man to win the heavyweight title. His 30-year boxing career fetched him close to $80 million.

At 46, he started promoting the Lean Mean Fat Grill Machine. This venture made him far more money than he ever made in the ring.

George is only one of numerous examples.

It is not too late to BREAK THE GLASS CEILING

In January 2006, at the age of 67, Ellen Johnson-Sirleaf became the first female head of state in Africa.

Despite previous political setbacks, she refused to give up. Her nickname "Iron Lady" comes from her iron will and determination.

In 2011, she was one of three joint recipients of the Nobel Peace Prize.

Born in Chennai, India in 1955, Indra Nooyi in 2006, became the Chairperson and Chief Executive Officer of PepsiCo, which is today the world's second largest food and beverage company by net revenue. Today, she is acknowledged to be one of the world's most powerful women in the business world.

Rania Nashar became the first female CEO of a listed Saudi commercial bank when she was named chief executive of Samba Financial Group in February 2017.

It is not too late to STEP OUT OF THE MOULD

Renew Your Mind. Small thinking or mediocrity has a way it downsizes our expectations, goals and aspirations. Move away from obstacle-focused, barrier-centric thinking and living, to a summit-reaching, growth and goal-getting mindset and lifestyle.

Like Matthew Ashimolowo, Global President of KICC, author and entrepreneur says, *"Get rid of the grasshopper mentality."*

Stepping out of the mould means coming out of the conventional or status quo..

Change the "Poor Dad" mentality. In Robert Kiyosaki's best-seller book *"Rich Dad, Poor Dad"*, he talks about breaking out of the stereotype of working for money and instead to make money work for you.

Dree Hemingway, an American actress, said, *"I think my biggest learning experience is that it's okay to be who you are - you don't have to exactly fit the mold of what people think a certain kind of career is."*

Stepping out of the mould also means **stepping out of your comfort zone**.

Here is a poem (author unknown) that captures this thought:

> **I used to have a comfort zone where**
> **I knew I wouldn't fail**
> **The same four walls and busy work**
> **were really more like jail.**
> **I longed so much to do the things**
> **I'd never done before,**

But stayed inside my comfort zone
and paced the same old floor.
I said it didn't matter that I
wasn't doing much.
I said I didn't care for things like
commission checks and such.
I claimed to be so busy with the
things inside the zone,
But deep inside I longed for
something special of my own.
I couldn't let my life go by just
watching others win.
I held my breath; I stepped outside
and let the change begin.
I took a step and with new strength
I'd never felt before,
I kissed my comfort zone goodbye
and closed and locked the door.
If you're in a comfort zone,
afraid to venture out,
Remember that all winners were
at one time filled with doubt.
A step or two and words of praise
can make your dreams come true.
Reach for your future with a smile;
success is there for you!

It is not too late to EXERCISE YOUR CREATIVITY

In 1974, Erno Rubik, a Hungarian inventor, sculptor and architect developed a cube.

The Rubik Cube became the world's best toy – 300 million sold.

Erno was motivated by a fascination for space and its rich possibilities, which yearned for expression. He did not let the communist environment in which he lived stop him.

Anna Mary Robertson Moses, better known as Grandma Moses, began her prolific painting career at 78. In 2006, one of her paintings sold for $1.2 million. Previously, she was a housekeeper and farm labourer.

Like American television presenter, media mogul and philanthropist, Oprah Winfrey, said, *"It doesn't matter who you are, or where you come from. The ability to triumph begins with you. Always"*

As Spanish artist, Pablo Picasso said, *"The chief enemy of creativity is 'good' sense."*

Mary Lou Cook, an American actress, defined it as *"Creativity is inventing, experimenting, growing, taking risks, breaking rules, making mistakes, and having fun."*

Elon Musk, Founder and CEO of SpaceX and Tesla Motors, says *"It's worth looking at industries which a lot of people think are impossible or think you can't succeed at - that's usually where there's opportunity."*

Today, opportunities to be creative abound. Sometimes, even the lack of some resources can bring out a person's creative genius in handling a situation or in solving a problem.

The impact of digital technologies has changed the dynamic in homes, organisations, industries, and societies. Disruptive technologies like the smartphone and social media platforms and channels have opened up to individuals and communities alike, a plethora of possibilities.

It is not too late to BUILD YOUR CAREER

David Blunkett was born blind in England in 1947. He was told he had limited career options because of his disability and should therefore consider becoming a lathe operator.

Contrary to expectation, he got into the University of Sheffield. He started his working life as a clerk/typist, then became a lecturer in industrial relations and politics; at 22 years, he became the youngest Sheffield councilor.

In 1987, he became a Member of the British Parliament. In 1997 he became the first blind cabinet minister in the country. In 2001, he became the Home Secretary (a senior cabinet position with responsibility for internal affairs in the country) - fulfilling an ambition.

Despite perceived handicaps, they should not become obstacles to progress.

It is not too late to FULFIL A LIFE-LONG DREAM

On March 17th 2008, Anne Poole passed the final part of her piloting test in a Piper PA38 Tomahawk, at the Highland Flying School to become the UK's oldest female pilot at the age of 65.

She said, "Spread your wings ... Don't put up your legs"

A 15-year old boy sat down at his kitchen table in Los Angeles many years ago and wrote three words at the top of a yellow pad, "My Life List." Some sixty years later, John Goddard had completed 109 of the original 127 goals he wrote under that heading.

His goals included climbing the world's major mountains, exploring from source to mouth the longest rivers of the world, piloting the world's fastest aircraft, running a mile in five minutes and reading the entire Encyclopedia Britannica.

John had not given up on completing the other goals, even as he added new goals to the original list. John died in 2013.

It is not too late to BUILD AN EMPIRE

Don't stop dreaming. Build an empire in your mind first because what your mind's eye cannot perceive, you cannot conceive, and what you cannot conceive, you cannot *receive.*

He had dyslexia, resulting in poor academic performance as a student. By the age of fifteen he had started two ventures that eventually failed. At

sixteen, he left school and began his first successful business – a student magazine. When he was seventeen, he opened his first charity, the "Student Advisory Centre".

Today, Richard Branson is one of Britain's wealthiest men, as founder and chairman of the Virgin Group of over 400 companies, including Virgin Atlantic and Virgin Media.

Jeff Bezos had a lucrative career in computer science on Wall Street and took on top roles at various financial firms before transitioning to the world of e-commerce and launching Amazon at 31.

It is not too late to CREATE A BRIGHTER FUTURE

Start with yourself. Have a clear vision of your future. Remember, your vision is your future. Map out a path of what you need to do to realise your dreams.

Then go on to touch other lives as well.

Peter J. Daniels came from a family of welfare recipients. Some were alcoholics and many had served jail term. He himself was academically challenged, failing in every year at school.

He became a bricklayer. However, his story does not end there.

With determination and a will to never give up, he is today one of Australia's wealthiest men. One of the most fascinating things he did to start the process of change was to become an avid reader. He taught himself not only to read, but went on to read over 6000 biographies. Today, he is touching countless lives around the world through his work as a life coach, professional speaker and renowned philanthropist.

Don't leave this planet without depositing what you entered with to help humanity. The graveyard is said to be the wealthiest place on earth – not some oilfield or diamond mine. The graveyard contains the remains of people who died with their unfulfilled dreams. Buried in it are leaders, inventors, educators, entertainers, authors and a host of other professionals and world changers that never were.

So start making a difference today.

Chapter 10

Avoiding Time Wasters

In today's fast-paced world, with its many and often competing activities, attractions and engagements, it is easy to get bogged down or involved in some things that have little or nothing to do with achieving your lifetime goals.

Even though some of these involvements that take up time may be outside your control, there are several others within your control that are worth mentioning.

They include the following:

- **Keeping wrong company**
- **Procrastination**
- **Interruptions by phone or in person**
- **Poor time management**

- **Lack of focus / doing too many things / no prioritising**
- **Poor planning and organisation**
- **Lack of knowledge or training**
- **Distractions / no discipline / daydreaming**
- **Fatigue or lack of concentration**
- **Being too helpful**
- **Wrong activities – reading junk mail, online chatting and unplanned continuous browsing and surfing online**

Let me elaborate a bit on each of the above points.

Keeping wrong company

The wrong company includes those who are gossips, idlers, mediocre thinkers, and sometimes even close friends and relations. Hanging out with or around such people or relying on their advice often has negative consequences, including a distortion of a person's perception, dampening of enthusiasm, slowing of progress, and in extreme cases, a complete abandonment of a life goal or dream.

Procrastination

Procrastination is a type of behaviour which is characterised by deferment of actions or tasks to a later time. Procrastination is a thief of opportunity. Procrastination will keep you from making tremendous progress.

Hara Estroff Marano, an award-winning writer and editor-at-large for the magazine *Psychology Today* says **"Procrastinators actively look for distractions, particularly ones that don't take a lot of commitment on their part."**

Interruptions by phone or in person

In a busy work environment, phones are likely to ring frequently. With the probable exception of telephone operators and receptionists, not all calls are important or demand immediate action. Without a clear plan for your working day, productive time can be sapped through attending to all phone calls. The scenario is the same with unannounced visitors, whether at home or at work.

With smart phones now commonplace, even more productive time may be lost through WhatsApp and other messaging and chat platforms.

Some of the ways to deal with frequent but unimportant phone calls include the following: keep the communication short or ask the caller to call at a time convenient for the recipient, or in the case of a repeated offender, to ignore the call altogether. Putting cell phones in silent mode during busy hours is a good excuse for avoiding unwanted calls.

Poor time management

A proper perspective of what constitutes a priority, something urgent or important as opposed to something unimportant or better handled or addressed by someone else will help overcome time management problems.

There is a false notion that effective time management is achieved when a person is able to do more in the same time. In reality, the ultimate goal of time management is to allow a person to do less work in a given time period without lowering the level of productivity - allowing for more time to do the things that will improve a person's life.

Lack of focus / doing too many things / no prioritising

Focus is the concentration of attention or energy on something. Without a focus, everything seems blurred. A focus therefore presupposes a clear vision. A broken focus will lead to an accident. Trying to do too many things at the same time or not prioritising often prevents a person from giving sufficient thought and devoting the right amount of energy and resources to what is paramount. As Bill Gates, one of the world's richest men, said, *"Only through focus can you do world-class things, no matter how capable you are."*

Poor planning and organisation

A chosen focus will determine the amount of planning and kind of organisation that will be necessary to realise a goal. In general, poor planning and preparation leads to poor performance. It is therefore important to be clear on what is to be achieved and to engage in the level of planning necessary to make this a reality. An effective organisation will reduce mistakes and the time needed to correct them.

Lack of knowledge or training

In management studies, much is made of the Experience Curve concept. The experience curve shows that the more experienced a person is, the less likelihood of making or repeating mistakes, leading to cost savings and ultimately giving that individual or organisation an advantage over others. The acquisition of knowledge and/or training will aid in getting this experience.

Distractions / no discipline / daydreaming

Distractions create delays for any person trying to complete a task or project. It takes some personal discipline to resist certain distractions, as these are seemingly pleasurable. These include watching too much TV instead of reading some educative or inspirational material, extended periods surfing the internet, long online chats and instant messaging, and daydreaming.

Fatigue or lack of concentration

Tired eyes and minds rarely see good opportunities. Fatigue leads to a slowing of the mental faculties and a loss of concentration. A shower, nap, rest or even a vacation can reinvigorate the body's functioning capability

Being too helpful

Setting boundaries on how far one can be of assistance will help create a balance in a person's life. Such a balance leaves the person feeling fulfilled as opposed to a feeling of being expended.

Wrong activities

A host of other activities are also time-wasters. These include many unscheduled and often fruitless meetings and events as well as reading junk mail. It has been purported that reading all the junk mail a person receives can take up to a third of their productive life.

Avoiding or minimising these and other time-wasters will markedly increase a person's productive time.

Chapter 11

---❀---

Using Time Wisely

Until a person comes to the place of understanding the value of time, it will most likely be misused. A conscious reminder of the importance of time will usually lead to better stewardship and a proper utilisation of this resource. Using time wisely may include the following:

Freeing Up Time

Instead of trying hard to keep facts and other data stored in one's brain, it is more prudent and time saving (in the long run) to write things down or log them in an organiser.

Writing down your thoughts and plans gives a permanent reference point for review and is also useful for monitoring your progress and for developing ideas.

Free up your brain from unnecessary tasks so that you can THINK CREATIVELY and WORK PRODUCTIVELY

Archive (store away) information that you do not need to recall from memory.

Make good use of your smartphone's features.

Having a Plan

In using time wisely, it is important to have a plan. As conventional wisdom has demonstrated, "every enterprise is built by wise planning."

It is important to set priorities on a TO-DO List. A system of priorities helps you keep your focus on what must get done.

Learn to distinguish between Projects and Tasks. A project is a set of activities carried out to meet some future goal. A task is the activity or job that needs to be executed immediately.

Today's smartphones have diary and calendar apps that can help in time allotments and management.

Managing Your Workload and Workflow

In managing your activities and workload, one should avoid taking on too much. It is important to first identify the MUSTs (what must be done), followed by the SHOULDs (what should be done), then the COULDs (what could be done) and finally the WAITs (the activities or tasks that can wait)

It is also important to realise that doing the right thing at the wrong time makes it the wrong thing.

Better outcomes will result from managing our own workflows properly.

Learning to Say NO

You can't do everything; neither can you please everyone.
Your chosen focus determines the world you create for yourself.

Nido Qubein, President of High Point University in the United States and also Chairman of Great Harvest Bread Company, said,

"Nothing can add more power to your life than concentrating all your energies on a limited set of targets."

Have you counted the cost of DIY (Do It Yourself)? As great as the concept may be, it may not always be worth your time to sort everything by yourself.

The principle of delegation and strategy of outsourcing arise out of this understanding. It is not everything that you have to get involved in. Some things are best left to others to handle so that you can concentrate on that which is paramount to your future. Learning to say NO can also protect your integrity, saving you from causing disappointments, which result from taking on too much.

Being Productive, Not Busy

As the great Greek philosopher Socrates said, ***"Beware of the barrenness of a busy life".***

It has been said that, ***"It is not so much how busy you are, but why you are busy".***

Paul J Myers, of the Success Motivation Institute, puts it well when he says,

> **"Productivity is never an accident. It is always the result of a commitment to excellence, intelligent planning, and focused effort."**

SECTION 3

GOING FOR OPPORTUNITIES

We have so far looked at how to get started on the journey to creating a future of success as well as how to prepare for opportunities. It is pointless, however, to get yourself all fired up and not know what it is you are looking out for or going for.

This third section, which comprises of 5 chapters, sheds light into what is needed to give us the successful outcomes we all desire. We will be looking at probably the most exciting aspect – using opportunities and creating opportunities.

Chapter 12 presents "*Using Opportunities*", showing us why we do not have to wait for something to be given to us on a silver platter. **Chapter 13** uses a story to show that "*Life is a Giver of Opportunities*". **Chapter 14** on "*Opportunities and You*" explains how to use what you have to turn on the ignition for your drive through the roads of opportunity. **Chapter 15** explains the how of "*Creating Your Opportunities*" even when life does not appear to present you with any. **Chapter 16** presents keys to "*Winning in Life*".

There is a saying that *opportunity comes knocking on your door*. This is possible, but is not usually the case. If you are to live the life of your dreams, you will have to go after opportunities.

It has often been said that a journey of a thousand miles starts with a single step. In going after opportunities you will need to take some steps.

These steps, building on from a good mental preparedness that we discussed earlier *(namely success mindset, right attitude, proper perspective, and a good expectation)*, are your decisions and corresponding actions.

Contrary to what is commonly said about opportunities coming but once, life presents us with many opportunities to reach our desired goals and fulfill our dreams.

It is important to walk or run with the following:

- **Develop a good work ethic.**
  Working smart and also working hard. Make up your mind to be outstanding wherever you are. Go the extra mile.
- **Refuse to give up.**
  No matter the obstacle that crops up, there is always a way to overcome it. Never lose your determination and your faith.

- **Never despise small beginnings.**
  Don't compare yourself to someone else who seems to be way ahead, as we each have a unique course or chosen endeavour.
- **Understand the power of networking and team working.**
  No one can reach the height of success without help from others. Seize given opportunities to work with and relate to others who have high values.

Chapter 12

Using Opportunities

Indecision is the thief of opportunity. The often temporal nature of opportunities necessitates capitalising on them as soon as they become available or present themselves. Indecision can lead to the loss of such opportunities.

Sun Tzu, a legendary Chinese general, said, *"Opportunities multiply as they are seized."*

Waiting for the most favourable situation or convenient condition may be a costly mistake. Strike the iron when it is hot.

It has been said that *"Doors of opportunity don't open, they unlock; it is up to you to turn the knob."* Most opportunities require some action or initiative or response from us. Waiting for it to be delivered to us on a silver platter may never happen.

William James, an American philosopher and psychologist, said, *"He who refuses to embrace a unique opportunity loses the prize as surely as if he had failed."*

Agnesë Gonxhe Bojaxhiu (more commonly known as Mother Teresa), the Albanian missionary who made a positive difference in the lives of many in Calcutta, India, said,

"Life is an opportunity, benefit from it.
Life is a dream, realise it.
Life is a challenge, meet it.
Life is a promise, fulfill it.
Life is an adventure, dare it.
Life is life, fight for it."

Chapter 13

---------- ❧ ----------

Life is a Giver of Opportunities

We can liken life to a race. Each of us has been given what it takes to make maximum impact in our given assignment on this planet, benefiting from the opportunities it presents us at the same time.

Going back to the tortoise and hare story mentioned in Chapter 3: the lesson from that race was that having a gift or talent was no guarantee of success. **Every gift or talent has to be put into use as opportunity serves so that we can get skillful at using it. It is our skillful use of these gifts and talents that will enable us make great strides towards the fulfilment of life goals.**

As great as this lesson is, it is only part of the story of the tortoise and the hare. In reality, there were three other races, each with its own important lessons – lessons to help us win in the race of life.

After the shock of losing the first race to the tortoise, the hare did some soul-searching on why he failed to win the race. He realised that being overconfident can be a dangerous thing.

He went back to the tortoise to ask for a second race, to which the tortoise promptly agreed, assuming that everything would be the same as before.

So at the agreed time and place the race started and the hare took off at top speed. This time, however, he did not give himself any rest, running at his best until he had crossed the finish line.

Of course, the tortoise was dumbfounded, not expecting the world around him to change. It was his turn to do some soul-searching, at the end of which he found a key principle of life: **being gifted together with having a sense of purpose and urgency is more beneficial than being gifted and taking things at snail's pace or for granted**.

He called the hare and asked for another race. The hare, who could not conceive how the tortoise could ever beat him, hastily consented.

On the agreed date, the tortoise asked the hare to meet him at a different location from that used in the previous races. When the hare arrived, the tortoise told him the specific point that would serve as the finishing line. The hare was not interested in any specifics. He was just raring to go. So the race started and off sped the hare.

What the hare did not know was that the tortoise had changed the race course to one where he, the tortoise, could have an advantage. So running at top speed, the hare arrived at the bank of a small river in record time only to discover he could not complete the race as the finishing point was across the river and he could not swim. The tortoise eventually got to the river, swam across, and completed the course, even though at snail's pace. The hare, understandably, was furious.

The lesson from the third race is that even with your gifting, **you have to choose your playing field to make the maximum impact.** Take your skills where they are valued. It could be to a different firm. It could also take you away from where you might be geographically based. It could be that the way you use your gifts and talents needs some modification. I like to think of it like a chef who uses the same main ingredients to create dishes and delicacies, each of which appeals to a different audience. The appeal often comes from the way these are presented.

In life, when faced with failure, sometimes it is appropriate to work harder and put in more effort. At other times it may be more appropriate to change strategy and try something different. There may also be times when it is appropriate to do both.

Coming back to the hare and tortoise story, both of them talked things over after the third race, and decided to run a final race. This time though, they would help each other.

Using the same course as for the third race, the hare sped off with the tortoise on its back. When they got to the river bank, the tortoise put the hare on its back and swam across to the other side. Then the hare put the tortoise on its back again and sped to the finish line. As you might expect, they finished the course in record time. Both were filled with glee at their remarkable performance and in crossing the finishing line together. They both felt a greater sense of satisfaction that in previous races. What a great ending, with an important lesson too.

Teamworking and the Power of Networking

There is power in working together. No matter how skillful a person is, there are areas where others probably do better. Synergy is created when individuals work together, compensating for each others' weaknesses with their own strengths. Even more important are the outcomes, which are greater and better than the sum total of the individual achievements.

Networking helps to extend our reach. Successful people have relationships that help to open doors for them, support them to achieve more than the ordinary, and to live the life of their dreams.

Who are you connected to? Yesterday's associations are by-gones. Today's relationships may be great for the moment but may not take you to your desired future.

Find the people who stretch your thinking - who don't just point out your faults, but help you overcome them. These are the ones who stand with you as you face challenges and applaud you as you overcome each one. They let you know that you are greater than where you're at today. They keep reminding you of who you can become.

Chapter 14

Opportunities and You

Every living being has a talent or unique gifting that is designed to make life meaningful. Even though animals are of a lower order than humans, I cannot but help notice how each species is uniquely and appropriately designed.

Take for example, an eagle with its clear vision as it swoops upon its prey from great heights; or a rhinoceros' keen sense of smell, allowing it to recognise danger even from miles away; or a dolphin that can tell friend or foe from detecting and projecting ultra sonic frequencies. Each of these creatures, by a natural process of mentoring and/or experience, perfected the use of their given arsenal.

No human being is devoid of talent. The starting point is to discover **what gifting or ability you possess**, whether innately given or acquired, and to develop and perfect it.

It is important to note, however, that ability alone will not guarantee success in life. What will need to be added is a **passion in employing that ability**. That means using the given skill, gifting or ability even when it appears inconvenient or does not bring any material rewards. Passion produces staying power for the journey of life.

Passion refers to that innate and/or burning desire to accomplish something. To each one of us has been given that which we are passionate about. It could be somebody's pain that you feel. It could be a situation that makes you unhappy and which you would want to do something about. Not everyone will share your passion about something.

Attraction brings something to a person's attention, but it is passion that will keep the person interested. This interest leads to a desire to do something about it, which in turn leads to some action being taken. For instance, some are concerned about the plight of the homeless, some others are concerned about orphans, others still are concerned about youth and teenage crime, the criminal justice system, poverty, ignorance, and a host of other issues.

Finally, having **a whole-hearted and life-long commitment to excellence**, in addition to talent and passion, will create opportunities and ultimately a better future. Make a decision today to do away with whatever is average or mediocre in your life by adopting a mindset for excellence.

As Vince Lombardi, an American football coach, once said, *"The quality of a person's life is in direct proportion to their commitment to excellence, regardless of their chosen field of endeavour."*

Chapter 15

Creating Your Opportunities

George Bernard Shaw, an Irish playwright, said, *"The people who get on in this world are the people who get up and look for the circumstances they want and if they can't find them, make them."*

Orison Swett Marden, an American writer, said, "Don't wait for extraordinary opportunities. Seize common occasions and make them great. Weak men wait for opportunities; strong men make them."

Champions make decisions that create the future they desire. The quality of our decisions determines our outcomes and/or the consequences for our future.

You create your opportunities by asking for them. Even though preparation can position a person for opportunities, there are times when the opportunities have to be pursued.

Creating your opportunities will require making some decisions and investing your time.

It is important not only to make some decisions now, but to make the right decisions. This is because the decisions you make today will determine your tomorrow. Your tomorrow is the future you desire for yourself, your family, your organisation, your community, or your country.

Decisions are the starting point to creating your future, but without an investment of time to work on critical areas in your life, only limited progress will be achieved. An investment of time is a reflection of the value placed on something. Only after such a disciplined exercise will a person discover, develop and utilise their abilities, talents and gifting in a recognisably advantageous way (based on perceived opportunities) to create a brighter future.

A proverbial quote says that *"a man's gift will bring him greatness"* and *"a diligent man will stand before people of influence".*

Let your skills, abilities, decisions and diligence bring you into prominence, greatness and influence.

Chapter 16

--- ❖ ---

Winning in Life

Break Up Your Fallow Ground

Change your thinking and change the way you have been doing things. As a man thinks, so is he. Think productivity. Think value. As you change your thinking, it will change your perception and eventually change your actions. As has often been said, *"It is only a mad person that does the same thing and expects different results."*

Invest

An investment of time, money, energy and talent is the seed to a bountiful harvest of fulfilment and success for the future.

Prepare

I once heard success defined by a participant during one of my corporate training sessions as *"preparation meeting opportunity"*. It underscores the importance of preparation. *Preparation refers to an orderly combination of activities and behavioural patterns to achieve some desired outcomes based on some anticipated set of conditions or scenarios.*

Harvest

One of the key principles found in this life is the law of seeding and harvesting. Farmers probably understand this concept better than most others. What may not be so apparent to most people is that farmers have a virtue that others often lack, leading to short-changing themselves. It is the virtue of patience.

In today's fast paced, micro-wave results-producing environment, this virtue is often lost on many. There is an adage among the Creole-speaking populations of West Africa that says "*Patient dog go eat fat bone.*" It means patience will bring a good reward. Opportunities cannot be rushed. If an attempt is made to do so, it could lead to unsatisfactory results or undesirable outcomes.

Be like the farmer, who having done his work of breaking up the fallow ground, watering, sowing and nurturing, waits patiently to see the blade, then the ear, and finally the full corn in the ear, before harvesting his crop.

Wouldn't it be funny to see a farmer go dig up seeds sown each morning to see if they are germinating? He or she keeps expecting a good harvest, even when the natural elements seem to be contrary and all the while, he or she keeps doing what needs to be done – watering, fertilising, weeding and pruning to nurture, protect and maximise his or her bounty.

In like manner, keep doing what must be done – honing your skills, developing yourself, protecting your positive mental preparedness from contamination, and networking with the right people. Don't complain about the difficulties you may be facing in your journey of life. Instead, keep making affirmations about the kind of future you desire. Affirmations require you to speak out aloud the different positive things you desire and expect, even when faced with contrary circumstances.

As long as you have breath, nothing should stop you from speaking what you desire. The more you speak it, the more it gets inside of you and the more your faith and confidence rises. This increases your expectation, and eventually attracts what you desire.

**Your best days are
still ahead of you.**

Conclusion

Success can always be achieved as long as a person never quits trying to reach a goal. Yes, you might have some setbacks, but that should not stop you. Winners are not those who never fail, but rather those who never quit.

Read the story of Maxcy Filer who took 25 years and 47 tries before he passed the California Bar exams on his 48th attempt in 1991 at the age of 60. He said it was *"perseverance, perseverance, perseverance"* and that *"I was going to take it until the last inch of my breath."*

Or take the story of my good friend Mike. Mike's father left home, leaving his mother to fend for him and his siblings. With her limited income from selling in the local market she was only able to give her children an elementary school education. That seemed to be the end of the story where education was concerned for her kids – but not for Mike.

Mike befriended some boys in his neighbourhood that had the opportunity to attend high school. When they came home from boarding school on holidays, Mike would borrow their school books and read, teaching himself as best as he could. This practice continued for a few years until Mike registered himself as a private student to take the GCE Ordinary Level exams, normally taken after attending five years of high school in the British education system.

He passed the exams and went on to study commercial subjects at a polytechnic. During his brief tenure at the polytechnic, he did not depend on his teachers to spoon-feed him, developing the skill of self-tutoring. Through a series of positive steps, sheer determination and faith, Mike became the Operations Advisor for a global NGO – responsible for a region covering some dozen countries and as well as the Head of Audit Services for the whole of Africa and the Middle East. Today, Mike is pioneering new projects in Africa.

He holds two globally recognised professional qualifications in governance and auditing, as well as a postgraduate degree. Apart from the polytechnic education, Mike has not sat in a regular classroom session but studied and gained his qualifications through self tuition and distance education.

Maxcy Filer and my friend, Mike, were not competing with anyone. Opportunities are not races. It is not about getting to the end of a journey quicker than others. Rather, it is about completing a uniquely mapped out route and making the kind of impact the world is waiting for you to make.

In closing this book, I borrow a quote:

"The instruction you follow determines the future you create."

What kind of future are you going to create for yourself?

Opportunity beckons to You .....

Seize Your Moment

www.ingramcontent.com/pod-product-compliance
Lightning Source LLC
Chambersburg PA
CBHW072026040426
42447CB00009B/1744

Table of Contents

Astral Visions II

Super Channeling II

Secrets of the Galaxy

Astral Visions II

Wizard of Words

Once again you decided to step into the whacky domain of the wizard of words. What is it that draws you in again and again to hear the dew drops falling from the lotus? What is it within you that yearns to know the mysteries of Existence? Somewhere in your heart you will find your Home and realize that it is everywhere and that you have always been here. How relaxing to be welcomed by every blade of grass and every glint of starlight!

Who else but the wizard of words could wave his wand of wisdom and erase years of propaganda in a single stroke? Slice the Ego off, and all the pain which blocks the energy flow goes with it. Self-interest immediately limits you by associating you with limited time/place events, and very small-minded goals. One may attain their goal, but if it is at the expense of others, the miser has earned nothing more than a way to isolate their soul from others who might bring Love and Joy.

Focusing the third eye as high into the stream as possible, the wizard of words uses his fluid mind to paint pictures that bring you to a place that has always existed within. It is easy to do when you get to the point within yourself that is the same as the point within every body else. I am you and you are me. In your world, these words just happen to be appearing before your eyes. There are no coincidences, so for some reason this must mean something to you. It doesn't have to be a rigid concept. It could evoke a vague reminiscence.

Sometimes the Universe plays the wizard of words like an instrument through chakras resonating in harmony with the Aum. In the present moment unencumbered by interpretation, the perceptions which you-the-being receive through you-the-body suddenly pop to a whole new level. All the small petty concerns disappear because they never had any significance. Walk with grace and regard for Life, aware of each footstep and ye shall never fall, fail, or falter.

Each day the wizard of words discovers something fresh. Never will he allow patterns to set it, because the exhilaration of change suits his phoenix-like disposition. There is nothing left to do, but serve your natural purpose. Take the risk to allow the false imprisonments to be left behind. Forget fear by seeing that faith is a science of God. It is not simply a hope, but a guarantee when intent is met with the will to follow things through. Being productive every day brings happiness when it is an expression of your being. I'll tell you the truth, that if this is not how your life is, your soul is enslaved to circumstance, one of the most awful places to be. Waking in the morning to your imposed fate, the life juice drip drip drips away until the smile on your face is like pressing a button.

It is necessary to take on illusions directly and that is part of why the wizard of words came to this Solar System in the first place. Where he comes from, angels are by his side, and imagination instantly becomes reality. Hanging in space as a constellation with full mythological honors, sacred principles are stored in his experience. Millions of years old, he took an incarnation much as one might take a recreational drug. Once on the trip, you have to ride it out. The tricky thing about being here is that you get addicted and keep cycling through lives, perpetuating the phenomenon. The drama, the love affairs, the anger, the personal karmas…… Once you distance yourself from this, the Sun will fill you in on the next part. Some of you might not make it, but you can never say that you weren't exposed to some of the information that might have made your own salvation possible.

Welcome to the World

The information you need is now readily available. You must consider with your heart as well as your head activated by the eyes which so eagerly peruse. Sorting through the subconscious externalized as the internet, the keen mind knows that the Universe will put the appropriate materials in front of them. When read with openness to possibility, miracles of change become possible.

Recently arrived in body form, it takes many years to gain knowledge and then freedom from the same. Head in the stars and feet on the ground, the spirit conduit flows truth to all who will listen. We educate the children for the outer society, but the inner reality is barely mentioned. Our inability to answer even the most basic questions about life on Earth is not mentioned. Instead students are taught in absolutes, which distort their thinking for a lifetime.

Upon incarnating, the spirit should be welcomed into an environment of relaxation, dim lights, and lots of love. The wise adult guides the young one but never controls the exploration. Delight in God as He is so close. Watch the wonder and make it your own. Be humble enough to see the grace and beauty; do not impress your limitations upon the fragile flower.

Develop trust and friendship, while maintaining authority not by force, but by the sincerity of your convictions. Display in every moment the power of divine understanding. How you live tells volumes more than what you say. Many hide from wholeness, instead opting to maintain an intricate web of tangled contradictions. Splitting their psyche into many parts, the left hand never sees what the right is doing, and if the torso ever tries to tell either of the other, neither is open enough to listen.

Get back to a clean state of being. Consider every aspect of your existence again from the beginning. If you don't do it while alive, you will be forced to when you die. It is called the life review. Deal with the pain while you can heal and let time put it behind you. The Universe obviously knows what you are up to, and having set the parameters for this experiment is more than willing to forgive if you come clean.

Wisdom is Everywhere

With absolutely everything at your disposal, it is important not to be overwhelmed, but to start somewhere and wander around. Slowly you begin to realize what is happening and that although you have spent most of your life in a daze, when illumination is applied, everything falls into place. Give the process time and be patient with your own development. The problem is often in perspective, not in willingness to apply effort.

Your energy begins as a singularity, and then bifercates as it enters into this dualistic land. Symmetry is beautiful because it means you've fully materialized. Some people may appear unique and wonderful, while others may show the karma of past lives in their inability to sustain a healthy form. Some need to be hugged so hard their insides crack and the dark prison finally lets in the sunlight that they forgot they loved.

Read on as if you know not what I am referring to, but we all have to carry the burden until kneeling to the creative force. Somehow feeling ourselves responsible for the natural way of things, we over-blow our required duties and undermine our ability to soar unencumbered. Then we reinforce this foolishness in each other until someone sees for themselves the reality and awakens a friend.

A map is necessary. Nothing more; nothing less. One would be foolish to turn down assistance, and they would also be unwise to abdicate personal responsibility. Keeping balance above all things, a spirit warrior is free to dance as they please. It is okay to indulge and delight. These things teach you the deeper joys of non-attachment.

The wisdom you seek is everywhere. There is urgency as your body will die, but there is eternity for the soul to find salvation. The question is whether the 'one you are' will maintain continuity or not. If you cultivate consciousness and conquer fear you might have a chance. If you deny truth, then the pain of death will shock you into oblivion. Some of you will find ways to survive, but you will never be who you are now.

Armageddon of the Mind

Though we may see Armageddon in the outer
world, the inner condition which brought it on is
far more intense. The cosmic tug of war between
light and dark is fought inside the mind of
humanity and is merely reflected externally. The
images on TV of this occurrence may strike fear
into our heart, but is it not merely showing us
what lurks in our own subconscious?

Angels of Truth have sounded and Demons of
Darkness are struggling hard to hold their
deceptive ground. Some humans consciously
choose to ascend in light, while others grasp
tightly to their Denials and shout, "I want it my
way!" Heavenly friends may hurt for those who
harm themselves, but they should not let it stop
them from walking on inspired by Love from/for
their Creator.

The winding 'this and that' path becomes straight
and paved with gold when you realize that the
destination is each step and the glow on the
horizon is there so you know you are not alone.
Flowing through invisible bonds between your
Soul, the Sun, the Earth, and the Moon, the Aum
melts away barriers, releasing enough starlight to

fill the entire Universe. A living constellation, you can write your own mythology.

Old ideas fall away and the implications of a crumbling edifice may take a few moments to settle. Pain of loss is fostered by emotional attachment to stagnation. For awhile we were allowed to believe that things had stopped, but borrowing from our own future, it was intrinsic to the situation that the explosion of pent up energy would inevitably seek its freedom.

Suffering is necessary and for awhile it had to be so. When the edges have cut you deeply enough to crack the mental prison and let the long awaited morning arrive, shadows flee, and the frozen places begin to melt, shedding tears to release the frustration. Deep breaths and inner hugs transform the ache to ecstasy and the joy of life becomes awakened, never to be lost again.

The Miracle of the Mystical

Words are thrown about in a million ways about a million things, but those which contain the most magic are the ones that bring you back to yourself and engage the release of energies that have lain dormant in the soul for aeons. A person may mistakenly seize upon one form or another and draw conclusions based on their own preconceptions, but that will not change the inherent fact that Truth cannot be captured because it is an evolving reality with a tangible existence of its own. We can however, align ourselves with this Change and evolve with it.

The most basic understanding that begets the beginning of the process which leads to sublime fluidity is to realize that you are not simply this tiny body in this small mind. A false premise imprinted at birth by the deeper layers of the subconscious says, "I am a 3D manifestation". We tend to look at the world and reference ourselves based on the experience accrued from the age of Zero to Now. This includes influence from parents, hometown, love affairs, jobs, conflict, sorrow, and suffering. Release from limiting self-definition allows mental rigidity to loosen and newly freed past reveals amazing lessons about where you have come from and where you are going.

To enable this unraveling, one must surrender resistance to the ascension process. No individual knows the intricacies of another's unique personal journey, but encouraging the seeker from within the Universal Love behind Illusion, another who has already undergone the transformation, can share useful information about the type of things one might encounter along the way. Validation of experience is necessary so that the cosmic traveler does not start to feel crazy, and accept judgments of others that this in fact the case!

There are so many fantastic and transcendent experiences that can enter when Space is provided in the Heart. You must not perceive THIS according to the mental plane. YOU MUST NOT PERCEIVE THIS ACCORDING TO THE MENTAL PLANE. YOU MUST NOT PERCEIVE THIS ACCORDING TO THE MENTAL PLANE. YOU MUST NOT PERCEIVE THIS ACCORDING TO THE MENTAL PLANE.

Zen is our Destiny

Ancient mythologies of the world must be seen for what they are if a workable solution to the planetary situation is ever to be found. Within the context of a limited set of parameters, a cosmically palatable flow can never be given birth because it is intrinsically opposed to the expression of life – THE NEW. Just being old seems to give words credence in the mind of humanity. The older something is, the easier it is to lose track of the cause which creates the effect.

So much of what Jesus said is rooted in Existence and indicative of divine expression. Studying this Zen Master of the West, we can discover for ourselves the depth of his realization by practice of our own. The most harmful and anti-Jesus thing anybody can come up with, is to claim that belief alone is enough. Beautiful discussions on his seeds of truth again and again get cut down at the root by this simple but horrendous misunderstanding. There is no cosmic equation whereupon Jesus took your Karma. He provides tools with which to deal with your own Karma. The intrinsic nobility of ascension is that it is our personal responsibility to build a path to God. There is no escaping this process, and it is good!

15

Jesus is so much more than most Christians will ever know.

Muslims see the discrepancies of Christians, but unfortunately they are positioned squarely within their own subset of misconceptions. After being unacknowledged and abused for many years, they have rage and a desire for revenge. One cannot simply demand that this volcanic expression of Lost Will stop, because it will only polarize sides and escalate conflict. There has to be a safe receptacle for the subconscious lava to flow into, making room for peace. Within this tradition is an acceptance and understanding of the Mystical that can rise higher, unshackling itself from the societal conformities of any given era, and becoming universal in its embrace of moving reality.

Judaism is one of the planet's longest and most ingrained habits. Adherents claim to be God's Chosen People, causing enmity in those that they by definition oppose – everybody else. Moses was a law giver, not a truth giver. Even if it is taken on faith that the mighty stone tablets were necessary to establish order in the desert, to believe solely in this today, one would have to think that God is unable to grow and unable to communicate an updated message that would actually make sense to the situation NOW. Also, most claims of Jewish descendants for land and justifications for HARSH actions come from the Old Testament which itself was written by their own ancestors.

If one were to remove these three religious notions, most of the current wars would immediately lose fuel, politics would drop its wicked bite, and Planetary Peace as a World of Human Beings would suddenly be possible. Over the years attempts to get this point home have been met with such hysterical resistance that momentum for the cause periodically ebbs. The beauty of a real solution is that nothing of value is lost and all we held dear is set free to become the full fruition of what it was meant to be.

Zen needs no belief. It is an antidote to poison and the key to becoming centered. Getting space within is the only way to calm the turbulent waters of Earth's Geopolitics. Transforming the small "I" body into the big "I" soul, we serve the Tao, not Bush, Osama, or Sharon. This is where the brainwashing comes into stark focus. Answering the call of our own heart, we see that all this outside nonsense has nothing to do with us other than to throw us back to ourselves. Being immersed since the beginning it is hard to find the way out, but when you do, you will stand on top of the hill and shout, "Alleluia! This is it! The miracle we have all been waiting for has happened to me and can happen to you.

On Top of the World

What is it like to be on top of the world? Why
don't you ask yourself, or have you forgotten
what your feet are upon? Sure there may be a
floor, a bit of carpet, or some such thing, but just
beneath is the sheath of the planet Earth.
Radiating outward is the energy pumping from
the Heart of the Earth herself. Not to be denied
she Loves in spite of misery and despite many
spitting upon her. Buddha's blessings were given
from the Earth through him to the people. This
reveals the true gifts of the Lotus Paradise.

So many colorful qualities in people! Share and
enjoy without forgetting who you are and what
you came here to do. Find your role in the
expression of Love in the Universe and fulfill it.
That is what you long to do. That is what you are
truly here for. Keep all the information outside
your sphere and manage it with awareness. Do
not ever let it in too deep, and never let someone
else, let alone a content controlled picture box, do
the thinking for you. Find your source of
inspiration and let it flow and flow and flow.

Do not hold on to pebbles and cry about never
finding gold. There are many different types of

energy exchanges. Make sure you are engaged in healthy relating. Learning what it is that is happening inside of you is a good place to start. We have not been educated all the way yet, and many teachers are stepping up to fill the void. They are out there. Seek them and listen to them. Do not let foolish pride keep you from healing. Some sacrifice a lifetime of joy just to not have to say they are wrong or they are sorry.

All is forgiven and all is as it should be. Come home to the temple inside of yourself. I know the noise of the outer world is tempting and tantalizing. It has been that way for ages and thankfully the depth and sanctity of your inner world has been waiting for you. There are many questions and they will all be answered in the realization of your being. There is purpose and meaning behind your existence. There is a dream to be awakened and a mission to be accomplished. It is a blessing to be here and be alive this moment.

Source, Soul and Body Glow

Powerful and true like the night of the full moon, the luminescence of creation invigorates both animate and inanimate objects. Everything everywhere is moving. If you focus your inner hearing to a point which pierces the veil you will hear the humming that always surrounds you. If you merge with this hum, it will overtake you and start playing your heart like a musical instrument. The pain of many lifetimes will be lifted and you will see your true purpose. If you can carry the memory back with you, you can strive to reach this full actualization in your every day life.

To reveal deeper truth in words one must either wax eloquent or twist in a way that is just unexpected enough to suddenly make room for something new. Once a person has been exposed to the greater reality, they never forget. Some sad souls choose to stuff the memory and trudge on in their mundane affairs as if their smile actually means something instead of taking the sometimes difficult steps of asserting their individual independence. Chit chatting about nothing with friends of the same ilk, the ache of their suffering sounds like a room of weeping widows.

Vibration shoots through the sun to the soul and into the body. You walk around glowing your secrets to anybody with the Eye to see. We can work our way backwards to the source even as the salmon swims upstream. As our muscles get stronger and our Will is emboldened by success, each moment of the journey forward compounds the intensity of the spirit to arrive at full expansion. Soon we are giving off our own hum as a result of the splendidly skillful manifestation of the implications of truth. Reflecting on the lessons of experience, each opportunity leads to a better one. Instead of a spiral down, our path begins to wind its way back up.

Interpretation is not necessary. Leave these words where they are because the devil in this case is not in the details. The harmonic resonance of the pace and encoded geomancies lies beyond the reduction of meaning into the common lexicon. New pathways must be forged in order for transcendent potentialities to be revealed. Let's start with wherever we are in this moment.

Hopeful to be helpful, with the inescapable desire to reach the brightest star, a soul with the courage to make the mission their own will never fail if they never falter in their faith. It is not difficult to pour water through an empty tube, nor is it hard to get a bird to sing in the morning. For emerging heroes born to guard the truth, to be one with life and creation is as natural as it is for a baby to seek the warmth of a mother's embrace.

A Key to the Fountain of Information

Those who hold a key to the fountain of information can unlock the dream from the concrete cage and restore the shimmering luster that was once commonplace upon the Earth. Waiting for something to change is foolish when change is the nature of the Universe! The illusion is "that which stays the same". Much as people like to believe in their own self-identity, in the politics of their favorite government, or in the holy dogma that keeps their soul from being born, it is an effort in futility. These false idols will be stripped away because they only relate to the 3rd dimensional small world of incarnation in the Body/Brain.

Sure, to those trapped in Hell, Heaven seems very scary. They see subversion in freedom because they do not realize that the most dangerous technique of Control is to masquerade as Liberation. No eternal happening takes place solely in the Body/Brain. The Body/Brain can be used as a device to translate cosmic experience into words in an effort to shake the psychic self flagellators into taking it easy for a second or two, but this is always simply a means to a greater end.

Feeding off of the pain, Devils take themselves farther and farther into the dark unconscious hole of woe. "Come HERE!!!" they shout. "Why are YOU doing this to me?" Beware mon frere! This is how they catch a tiger by the toe and turn him into lunch meat. Demonstrate resistance by dancing; elevate existence by laughing. No one will awaken before their time, but those who fail to make it their time will be lost without a trace.

As if we are all helpless HERE..... What is the best case scenario? All wars, violence, lies, hammering propaganda, and dead wrong values disappear and a more enlightened, balanced, sincere, and loving world that implements already discovered scientific principles to the benefit of all humanity is one example. First a flag must be planted where you are standing. Lifting ideals and sharing the divine world WHICH ALREADY EXISTS is the first step.

A shift of focus must occur. I remember a "Simpsons" episode where living corporate logo characters were tearing up Springfield and the only thing that saved the town was a song with the message, "Just don't look. Just don't look." Every day when the sun rises, the birds sing outside of your bedroom window. It can be translated this way, "Glorious human, this is your lucky day. God has given you the gift of life for you to do anything you want with. This is your Home and you are Loved. Join us in the Garden to express your Joy."

Love, Peace, Friendship, Honor, Loyalty, and Truth

The prophets of old were speaking of something which the new sages have known for ages. Simply sitting on a shelf for 1000 years does not in any way add validity to a tome. Every word must be examined for pertinence to the present. Anything that binds is sowing seeds of discontent, while that which frees remains self-evident.

Finding gold in the most likely of places, Heart pumps out Love energy to the ends of the Earth. Those who have refined their taste to this delicacy of the Spirit will not be disappointed for spending the time sorting out the idiosyncrasies. Where each of us is right now, there is a key which can awaken the ability to perceive beyond the physical world represented by the cumulative impression of our 5 senses.

You cannot get used to that which is always changing. Mind reflects in concrete terms, while the motion in fact never stops. Buzzing atoms continue to mold to various forms due to certain properties of Physics. Try gazing blankly instead of focusing intently. Seeing all, we include the slice we used to know with the perspective of the whole.

Those who seek fear so they can worry and feel like they are doing something must beware of your habit. Drawn to paranoia, one can forget the happy world of nature and replace it with the monster around every corner. Good news is more thrilling than bad when you prioritize understanding over sensation. You focus on what you resonate with.

Once limited context is gone, your third eye will begin to reveal the next higher layer of the universe superimposed over the one with which you are familiar. A mere thought of a spirit will draw it near, and you will begin to get messages for those around you. Delivering them may give you hardship as you often run straight into fear, but over time the necessary difference will be made.

Things get really interesting when you can put your Will behind your Vision and Manifest a Reality which contains Love, Peace, Friendship, Honor, Loyalty, and Truth.

Harmony, the Golden Prize

To pull the Chi up from my toes and explode it out of my head only requires a mind that is free of distraction, a heart that is open and flowing, and an energy system resonating chakras in harmony with one another. Then while connected to the Earth and through her to the Sun, and beyond this to a space of Christ Consciousness unbounded, I can rain the truth down to the drought stricken dust of impoverished souls. Drink deeply; this will make room for many more and greater revelations.

A key to being receptive no matter who you are is to not allow the outer circumstances to cause you to justify acting as if faith is not enough to make all things possible. The journey may become trepidatious and fraught with unforeseen challenges. This spurs the hero on to greater triumphs while it disheartens the weak and those not self-loving enough to feel worthy of their rightful place in the house of the Father. Hold on to the image of what you want to Create and make sure every step is in that direction. If you are wandering all over the path, there is nothing wrong in it, but the consequences must be accepted as your own. The Universal laws are all

right out in the open for anybody brave and quiet
enough to take a look.

Ideas are wonderful and kindness towards
friends is even better. Do people smile when they
see you coming? What happens on their face
when they think of you? This reflection when
viewed honestly can become your best teacher.
Learning the lessons of life is an ongoing process.
Class is never over and the day will not come
when there will be no more knowledge to
acquire. The growth of expansion is the essence
of who we are as beings of Light. The
circumstances we encounter are the triggers that
give us the opportunity to activate this essential
truth. What fulfillment at overcoming doubts
and hesitation! Being aware of who you are,
coming to terms with reality is not far behind.

Shed tears and be done with the past. Shed fears
and be done with the future. Sink in as deeply as
possible to this moment. Even these words
become nothing more than a link for you to be
here and now. Come into your home; feel what it
is like to illuminate the body with the soul.
Encourage the vibration to increase and let your
attention ride the wave to new heights. Seeing all
around you at once with full insight into the
whole of existence, you are deadly silent and

powerful in your brilliant presence. This is the greater reality that awaits all who are ready. There is nothing off limits to one who is ready to risk their burden for the golden prize.

Awakening Souls Around the World

Join me in the stratosphere for a few breaths of fresh air. Unpolluted by incorrect thinking, the subtleties are not lost. In fact they are enhanced by the brilliance of newness that is deep inside all of life. Pristine like a spring rain, the fountain of youth is really the expression of God's Love. Drink deeply and rejuvenate your spirit. The journey is long and there are many obstacles along the way. With fortitude, friends, and faith, the chances of arriving at your goal are greatly enhanced.

There is a soul hanging around the body and in between can be much confusion. When focusing on the "I" of the body, the noise is in control. When focusing on the "IAM" of the Soul, you are in the freedom of space and can harmonize the noise into a symphony of creation. The Soul has a direct link to Source and when contacted can flow to you the truth of life and the meaning behind your own incarnation. Reading good books can enable you to more readily perceive the nuances of this Universal language.

To foster the release of the Soul seedling's potential, give it room to grow. When you hear the voice of intuition, remove the doubt that crushes it. Reality is far-fetched. You must allow your mind to wander to intricacies outside of your frame-of-reference. After all, you are trying to put the ocean into a glass. Luckily we don't have to put a lid on it, so the water can just pour all over the place. Allow yourself to giggle at the absurdity you suddenly realize was the case all along.

In one way, every day is like any other; in another, each is as different as the leaves on a tree. Creation is a composition called "Infinite Variations on a Theme of Life". If you listen closely enough, you will get to know the composer. If you open up to the energy and allow it to move you, it is very likely that you will add your own variations to the universal repertoire. In fact, we each play an irreplaceable role in this collective work of art. Even if you say you don't want to participate, at some point you made a choice to be a character in the play.

Embrace your role and dive into the performance. If acted in totality, all roles will be transcended and the grace beyond individuality will descend into your heart. Here you will see that you are all of the actors in all places. You've been so busy entertaining yourself in all your forms, that you've never stopped the drama to take a break. Just like a teenager with a new video game who stays up all night to get to the next level, you have been obsessed with seeing what happens next. It's alright, we'll all find out soon enough.

You Are Hypnotized

Pretty pictures fill the mind with delightful dreams. The system closes in upon itself and the associations made by flashing images creates an artificial reality much more comfortable than that which lies outside your door. It is easier to believe in cattle feed than to sort through the details of world history, psychology, sociology, art culture, and spiritual tradition to put together a view of life on Earth that includes the nobility of the soul creating its own destiny.

For those that think, "Yeah, I agree. Other people are really screwed up," consider that there is more than one layer of illusion. Even an adolescent can figure out that what is being portrayed by various media is ridiculously skewed. There are thousands of things in the background that are taken as a given that are not necessarily so. Societal context colors everything for those who have not traced their own life back to day one.

Remember all the facts and figures you were taught in school? How many of those ideas have been logged and forgotten never to be questioned again? Of course all the family values given to us by our parental figures are solid, right? Even the supposedly good creates an elaborate superstructure that clouds the effort to reach the ultimate truth. In fact this can be one of the most confusing temporary intellectual stopping points to overcome. Our attachments do not want us to pop this sacred bubble and although we may question some things, we can develop a blind spot that undermines us in subtle ways every day.

Further, there is a whole other level of basic worldly perception parameters that we may not have even considered. Do you notice colors, textures, tastes, sounds, etc..., and differentiate them into categories that then get stored in various areas of the brain? A reflective look takes this in, but does not allow the synapse grooves to interpret the occurrence into a more limited view. Of course we can acknowledge sense parameters, but there is no need to think about them, because as soon as we do, we lose the next moment.

Many forces on many levels work to pull us in a plethora of directions. People often adopt roles for changing situations that their mind proves to them is necessary. It is not. Only when arriving at our own center can we maintain consciousness amongst the wild activity of the jungle and its inhabitants. Consistency of self remains on an ongoing basis after the hierarchy of control mechanisms are dismantled with thundering awareness and truth is upheld by the courage to live as it is perceived from within.

As usual those who think they know fool themselves. There is much material to cover, but no concrete solution will ever be found. Information is digested so that when presented with a new circumstance we can be alert enough to spontaneously handle the situation. We can then take over the steering of the body-ship and chart new waters with a joy nowhere else to be found but in the expression of a heart that showers its love indiscriminately to the whole universe.

There is No Way Out But Through

There is never going to be an easier time to deal with that which remains to be healed. Hiding only delays the inevitable day of reckoning and adds to the life time wasted in misery. Why torture yourself like some deranged masochist when you can admit the truth, transform the energy, and set yourself free?

Imagine living in a hole, deep within the ground. You only allow yourself the smallest pleasure and even then you feel guilty. Sometimes it rains and sometimes the sun shines, but there is barely enough feeling left to take note either way. The goal is to merely survive; not to live, but to put death off a little longer.

Jump out of it! Do you think you have the luxury of complacency while the society…while civilization itself crumbles!? Forget the frowns that are always ready to arrest the truth. Those faces are the ones that will "freeze that way" to their own eternal detriment. Ignore their grumbles and show them your smile. There are always a couple of people who are ready to join in. Then together they can add more and so forth…

When enough of us join the party, our celebration can be organization. We can hold up signs of protest (which are necessary in a limited sense), or we can put the best minds on the planet to work on real flexible lasting solutions to world conundrums. Purposefully affirmative methods will blow the polarizing demigods right out of the realm of ideas.

Should a country destroy cities, or provide medicine for the people? Should it help the best and brightest go through higher levels of university without crushing debt, or are there more imperial conquests to be embarked upon for the interests of not the nation, but the corporation? Somewhere, somebody is sitting in a penthouse board room on a pile of cash laughing at the peons who no matter how obvious things get, will just not think for themselves.

Covering the Achilles Heel of the Soul

Polarization is occurring on its own. We as human participants will just find ourselves on one side or the other. One side will be Unconscious and one side will be Conscious. It is impossible to sit on the fence.

As those heading towards the Conscious side will find out, the ultimate weapon of the Unconscious is to accuse the Conscious of "Hate" when they express the Emotions that have been frozen. Those heading towards Consciousness are sensitive and loving. An accusation of "Hate" comes as a terrible blow to a being of Light. Beware, for this is the ultimate tool of Control. We need to cover this Achilles Heel of the Soul with Thundering Understanding.

The Unconscious hate themselves and so draw that to them in the outside world. If the Conscious are there, the Unconscious will do things until "Hate" rises in the Conscious. When the Conscious responds honestly to their feelings, the Unconscious will then accuse the Conscious of "Hate".

For the Conscious this is debilitating. For the

Unconscious, it adds fuel to their fire. This is how they feed off the Conscious and keep them from growing. The Conscious are expressing honestly to approach the "real" which is a reflection of Love. For the Unconscious the "real" is what they fear the most. They will do anything to stop it from disturbing their Denial.

Love seems like Hate to the Unconscious because they Fear the Truth. The Conscious Hate to be Hated because they can't stand to be misrepresented, and that is the trap. Feeling compelled to clarify, they will be lured into the Unconscious's trap. Each explanation opens the door to more Denials. Consciousness's energy gets used up, and the Unconscious feeds on the pain.

You will see these divisions increasing all over. God is sorting out the weak from the chaff. All spirits will go where they need to go for what they need to learn. The shadows will lurk in darkness while the stars will take their rightful place in the sky.

Beyond the Mind Edifice

Magnificent words that come from higher
dimensions do not do any good if they are simply
processed in the mind and interpreted according
to disposition. How can Wonder enter into the
world of preconceived parameters? A good story
can be interesting, but only truly serves the divine
purpose if it awakens something beyond the
norm in the receiver of the transmission. To the
one who has lived only in the mind, the hardest
thing is to let go of the illusion of knowing and
the sense that they have to control their
environment. There are ways. The trick is to get
you to jump out of everything you have ever
thought life was all about. Kicking the human
children out of the nest, it is finally time for each
to fly on their own. Spelling out the details,
perhaps we can find a crack in the mind edifice to
slip through.

So much gets crammed into the 5 sense Earth
body that it shorts out. This can manifest as
mental illness as well as later…physical sickness.
All of your prescription meds are vain attempts to
alter the body/brain chemistry that excessive
mental input has destroyed. Trying to live out a
myriad of contradictions, all actions are

disconnected and serve no greater purpose. It is good that it takes time for prayers/intent to manifest. If everything people thought just appeared, we'd be doomed. Things will surely come around our thoughts if we hold them over time. We must untangle the goop that is stuck to our innards then with space and a fresh perspective, we can see for the first time see our life path and create something that will contribute to our own wellbeing as well as the peace of the planet.

Without the strain of other people's pain, your body attains a new health and ability to perceive subtleties. This then makes it possible for your Higher Self to fully enter in and the Two become ONE. Rediscovering everything over again without the taint of mind is a pure pleasure. What a joy to have full intelligence and the newness of sunrise in your heart! Each moment becomes a miracle and you give thanks not from repetitive habit, but because gratitude bursts from your soul. You realize so clearly what a gift life is and how precious every last being is... Even now I feel blessed to press each symbol key that unlocks the doors to the mysteries of the universe. Out of nothing comes something. Something when shared becomes something more. Dancing without reservation, the celebration is at long last joined.

Tales of angels and demons are entertaining and indicative of something that is in fact the case. The meaning and reality is quite different than anybody that simply lives in the mind can realize. Here is where the language of mythology points you to the abstract that stays abstract. The left brained prove-it-to-me people will always say that evidence is needed on their terms, but what to do if reality has its own way? Tell them to open up their hearts and embark upon the journey of discovery so they can see for themselves. Sometimes you may start a course for one reason and suddenly find out that destiny had altogether different ideas. Once addiction to linear thinking is broken, the multidimensional possibilities add a richness and dignity to humanity that will easily relieve the sting of admitting ignorance.

Wake up World!

Even as the political situation disintegrates, the cosmic community coagulates. The end of the Old World is taking place right alongside the beginning of the new. Looking elsewhere for the occurrence simply shows that the seeker has yet to realize the happening is here and now. There is no other place and time. 90% of the Souls who have ever been are once again alive in this era to witness a momentous event in human evolution.

We can call it the dawning of the Age of Aquarius or the Ascension into Universal Humanity. We can call it Spiritual Awakening or Meditative Enlightenment. Whatever name we ascribe to it, it is essentially Self-Awareness empowering Individuals to take over conscious creative control of their own destiny by connecting to the Source through the Soul. In this way Man's Will and God's Will become one and the blueprint for Existence becomes actualized. Those who think they have higher priorities residing in worldly affairs have grossly misunderstood the purpose and underestimated the significance of being on Earth.

When wrapped up in the details of personal

ambition, to look outside of self-identity at the truth of being on a planet in outer space seems too inconvenient. To consider your impending death....that's downright morbid! Or is it? What else is going to keep the razor's edge of Life in your Mind? Nothing crystallizes this tremendous gift of opportunity better than to realize that it will be gone one day. Shirking hesitation for exaltation, you become free to dive into yourself and release your natural talents.

The better you are, the better everything in your life will be. When work is necessary it can be done with a calmness and originality that wasn't there before. Relationships will become nourished by validations that are no longer left unsaid. Love no longer rests upon the shelf but becomes an everyday thing. The more you give the more you get in return. This is the Law of Abundance. The more miserly one acts, the poorer will be their spirit when the decrepit body finally returns to dust.

A clarion call is not nearly loud enough to reach ears that have been sleeping for lifetimes. If I could personally look into everyone's eyes and give them exactly what they need I would be happy to do so. Often this is not what the person thinks they need. The road home goes through the thorniest territory. When the horrible reality of the cage is first looked at, it is likely that the grumpy sleeper will blame the messenger. That is why the messenger has to be skilled at delivering the goods.

It is old news that Christianity is full of hypocrisy and its reptilian rituals were organized in Board Rooms, not in Heaven. Of course we all know that the loser in every war is Evil and the winner Benevolent, right? Nations with their borders exist everywhere don't they? Just look at that big black line floating in the sky between Canada and the U. S. Where does that crazy thing come from? Well, we all know we have to protect what's ours. Let's just get this over with, "MINE, MINE, MINE!" Once again we see that George Harrison was slipping us a gem, "All through your life, I Me Mine….."

Spoiled children don't deserve the Kingdom of God. Holding onto misery they cry, "Why won't He let me in?" The door has always been open. The punishment humans feel has been given to them by each other, not God. Take responsibility and stop whining. It is not such a big deal. The impossible will only become possible if you believe it to be so. Miracles happen every second of every day. Where have you been?

You Cannot Activate DNA Linearly

Shall we go over the rising vibrations on Earth
that even now lift us more into the mind of the
Sun? Perhaps we should explore how the Earth
mother and Sun father share their Love in the
expression of Life. We make our Heavenly
parents so very joyous when we become self-
conscious and appreciate with gratitude that we
are alive! Even if we were to examine the
implications of the Aum vibration that
invigorates both animate and inanimate objects,
we would never arrive at any conclusions. We
would possibly start to dissolve some illusions
however.

What if we were to talk about the scary
governmental machinations across the globe and
how they are but a reflection of humanity's
unresolved subconscious? After all, there is
something inside all of us which causes the
reflections we see. There is nothing but the
observer and that observer is the same in each
one of us. We mistakenly think it is "I", but this
"I" is every "I" and at some level is an "EYE"
which is fully aware of the multi-fercations and
the ONE simultaneously.

For those of you who might reply with some smart ass comment about lack of coherence or that I must have done some crazy drug to write such madness, you will never know. But what I can tell you is that YOU CANNOT ACTIVATE DNA CODES LINEARLY. Eventually we will highlight all the pieces. Do you see that in the now even reading becomes a different process? Only this word. Only this word. Only this.

We have had enough content that is 'ever so factual'. Is this really going to serve any purpose anymore whatsoever other than to bore our asses off and provide cover for the scary lunatics who aren't willing to take responsibility for anything? We all know that if you dare question an average American, the first thing they will do is blame someone else. Not even a pause for self consideration, so many have thrown away the Awareness key long ago because they mistakenly believe they know something. It is for absolutely nothing that you protect your misery.

What if a golden spoon appeared under a crescent moon? And upon this there was a cherry and it was said that this particular cherry if eaten would reveal everything that is necessary to solve all of the world's problems... Who would pop the tiny fruit of wisdom? And would all of those

left out of 'the know' ever acquiesce to the will of
the awakened? No doubt the newly christened
sage would hurt all of their feelings so much that
they would lynch him or her. But like many
sages before, they will keep on spilling the beans.

Hoots and hollers from the audience emerge
while true devotees make themselves known in
the most wonderful of ways. No one will reach
everyone, but if someone reaches someone else,
hasn't something been done? This is no
conundrum to be stuck upon, it is more likely a
form of proclamation that it only takes a gesture,
an expression, or the subtlest of winks in the
energy within your eye to make it known that
you are a part of creation.

A final point that must always be remembered:
Outer space is your inner space.

Discover Your Own Transcendent Truth

The truth is we can go farther and farther still. When we can finally conceive without conclusion that there is no stop, then we can fully enjoy the Go Go God. When at last it dawns on us that stagnancy is death, we will embrace the change and luxuriate in the rejuvenating influx that never ends. The question of how to link to Source is a simple one. It revolves solely around the efforts you put forth in facilitating the process through paying attention to what is occurring on an ongoing basis. People are not enlightened because they do not seek to be. Too wrapped up in pettiness and mundane affairs, they use up all of their energy and opportunity, finding peace only in an early grave. Even in this case the body rests in the dirt, but the spirit remains continually tormented. Human emotion is a type of drug for the addicted ghosts, often causing them to immediately leap into another body. An urgent newly deceased energy entity can even go so far as to draw a man and woman together by force of will from the astral plane to open an incarnation portal. This is particularly true where alcohol is involved. It makes room for the undetected entering of this influence.

The etheric double is not the Soul. It is the body's energy equivalent. This is what survives death with the personality still intact. So there you are in the astral realms first vibrations, which overlap with your former reality. Where you find yourself is really not that different from what you are used to...in some way more brilliant and fluid. Very dreamy and magical, it is actually a relief of many burdens associated with the body. Gravity is not as prevalent since the body is no longer there. You are light and free, traveling with but a thought and inclination. Soon you will encounter old friends and life goes on. For some who had a traumatic crossing that pierced into their mind and remained with them even after the physical passing, there is a period of rehab. This situation is monitored by guides and the equivalent medical/psychological assistance is available upon arrival.

The few individuals from Earth who had dismantled their Ego and personality imprint while alive will have another kind of experience entirely. The colloquial phrase which comes to mind in this case is, "The World's Your Oyster"; then apply what that phrase represents to the whole Universe. Some will share long visits with the entities which exist in the realms beyond form, space, and time. These beings have many experiences to share. It may take a million years, or a split second. Once you get this far you can jump in anywhere on the time line anyway, so it is irrelevant. Many who remember themselves to this point will assist evolution on planets here and there. Jesus and Babaji have agreed to be governors or caretakers of the blue-green planet Gaia. Some of the masters traveling through such as Buddha, Osho, and your author come from other star systems and have been around for ages. Take this chance to open to the vibrations available and discover your own transcendent truth.

The White Light of Star People

Where does it all come from? These words emerge out of nothingness even as every blade of grass springs forth from but a code intrinsic to the seed. Appearing and disappearing in time, all things are fleeting. I beg you to reconsider your conclusions. Behind every known is but another unknown. Pain comes from giving too much credence to temporary manifestations. Your being lives outside of these limited phenomenon. Your godlike nature transcends everything you can consider.

I'd love to rumble you from your toes and shake off the flaking paint from your personality wall's woes. Perhaps if I shimmy up to your ear and shriek a piercing pitch in a very disconcerting slightly wobbly tone, suddenly stop, look you straight in the eyeballs and whisper, "NOW THIS…" you will have a moment truly in the present. So many things that you haven't considered for so long lead you to falsely believe they are a permanent part of you. What does a new born baby see? Does it yet know the colors red, green, yellow, or does it differentiate between this and that? Does it even know that everything it sees is separate from itself?

Mind tends to embrace pattern, and after a pattern has been witnessed a number of times, it gets filed into the known category. This then dulls the perception of the new now when it is taken for granted that what is being seen has already been experienced. If you have been in the same room 1000 times, can you still see the magic and mystery bursting just below the surface? Looking in the mirror, do you smile about the fact that you are even here and how absolutely preposterous the whole notion is to begin with? If you asked even some of these questions and then went out into the world, no one would be able to transgress against you, because there would be no-one specific there to transgress against. You would see that you are a part of a flux that is in and all around you.

A few sources of information cross reference until they become a focal point for self-consciousness, but they never lose their connection to the heartbeat of existence. Even as you read this, wonderful things are happening. You are one whacky creature human! Walking around in your body, running things through your mind....what luxury you grant yourself! Patiently the Soul waits to recollect all the experiences of every incarnation. Then you can give yourself the 3rd birth into Christ

Consciousness. You are born again in the process of awakening, then when the mission is complete, you get born a third time. This is reuniting with the originator of the whole plotline. Here you will be free of all condensing concepts, floating in space and happy to remember what the whole thing was about.

I am so glad to reach eyes, ears, and hearts that care about such things. One by one star people are emerging and together we are turning the cacophony of suffering into a symphony of joy. Welcome to Earth my friends. It has taken awhile to go through the whole transformation, and I know it is perilous beyond compare. Thrill seekers who do the fantastic, are just playing around with the great thrill we all dared to take call Life. I honor you for your decision and strength. Every one of us here is already powerful. A little Black Magic has turned the easily influenced into sleeping dreamers, but a little White Light easily clears that up.

On the Path to the Christos

Standing at the threshold of incarnation, our Spirit gets ready to make the leap into the Time Portal with full Consciousness of what we are doing, and prepared to live out the life we have planned for ourselves with the assistance of guides and angels. Once in the Vortex to the 3rd dimension we start feeling the compression and for many this sparks an intense dread/memory of the forgetfulness they barely remember from their last attempt at embodiment. Soon this no longer matters as attention gets drawn to the body we are to inhabit. Finding ourselves in a womb, there is nothing to do but to breathe, and wait.

After a long steady period of growth and relaxation (that is if the mother doesn't smoke, drink, or eat rotten food), a rumbling announces that the next phase is about to begin. Suddenly we are being pushed towards a hint of light that has appeared from nowhere. Resistance serves no purpose and in short order we have emerged into the starkness of Life on Earth. The Love of a mother's smile instinctually relieves the baby of the initial terror and the road ahead begins.

The progressing child learns the ways of

humanity and adopts the mind-set of the culture. Constantly reinforced in this by those around them, they truly believe they are a person in a body for a bit of Time. They develop their mind and become more and more certain that they are who they think they are. But what is this feeling inside underneath it all? Simultaneous to the surface activity, there has been a dim but constant echo. Something inside feels that they come from God and that their own Existence means so much more than they yet know.

Reaching the limits of Mind, the aging aspirant draws to them a facilitator. With a hug of Love, the master blasts open the mental prison and for the first time the human discovers that they are alive! The heart bursts forth in song; gratitude and tears of Joy reveal that Life will never be the same. Making up for past transgressions, everything that is touched, now turns to Gold. The alchemy of inner transformation has begun.

Day after day upon awakening the newly found faithful friend to nature is happy to discover that they remember the world is a magical place. Assimilating the 4th dimensional astral plane, they are frequently transported to other realms to have experiences unlike any they have ever had before. Angels and ghosts, Eye beings and dragons, ancestors and famous artists you love, various gods and all the creatures of the elemental kingdoms will begin visiting from time to time. Door after door will open and all of your dreams are revealed as visions of a higher reality.

During this process of ascension the progressing disciple comes to know their Soul and through recovering it piece by piece will remember past lives and regain the experience of each one. Becoming integrated, new talents present themselves and through allowing them expression, they paint the road ahead. Experiencing, reflecting, and creating, the Heart opens wide and begins to stream in a never ending expansion of Love.

Lifting off of Earth consciousness which up to this point had been the Holy Spirit which had set things into motion, the Soul now realizes the Power of Wholeness, and consciously returns to the Path with full Awareness of all that has come before. Tuning into the Sun, the 5th dimension is attained and for a time you will be the representative of the Sun on Earth; or put another way, the Son/Daughter of God. Everything you encounter, you will shine your light on and lift to this level of perceptive capability. Free of the Mind and wrapping the Heart in Awareness, there is nothing in this place which can touch you. Settled in your inner aloneness, aware that all is One and that we are seeing but various slices of spectrums here and there, the Super Individual is ready to see even the known universe disappear and still be steady on their feet.

The secret history of the solar system is them revealed by the Sun itself. If you have found favor, the Sun will introduce you to other stars and through them you will communicate with beings on other worlds. Soon the whole of Space is your playground and Thy Will be Done on Earth as it is in Heaven. Sharing the Creative Force with the Great Creator, you become Ambassadors of Change, the Wellspring of Life. Ideas are toys/joys that you share as your fulfillment cannot but shower intricacies/delicacies all around. Eternity is just long enough to enjoy the potentials which can be explored.

After awhile the Archangels who have become your best friends start flying in a whirling circular motion over the top of your head. Suddenly, you have been lifted up and out by the vortex they have created. No longer bound to the Soul or this Solar System, you realize the full scope of who you are and always have been. The Christos is awakened. Your heart feels so juicy that it is oozing Love, and your mind is completely quiet. There is a Cosmic Holiness to the Universal Truth that is now your own Understanding. The messianic visions of youth were but a harbinger of the Second Coming of Christ which comes again and again in those few who truly go for the deepest meaning of Jesus' teaching. Gaining enough momentum to escape the gravity of this place, more friends and new experiences are waiting in many other parts of the Galaxy. You are free to go.

Super Channeling II

It is an Age Old Battle

Ye who art the keepers of darkness, take heed across the land.

The truth which has been guarded through the millennia by but a few human hearts, has survived the period of tribulation. Beginning to take deep root, the influx of resources from the astral plane has become a wave that will be impossible to stop. The ascension will and is going forward. All messages to the contrary are planted by those who adopt methods in attempts to deceive.

Furthermore it is quite possible to channel angels or demons. The demons will use similar and sometimes even more skillful language, but their cunning intent can be felt by the pure aura of one connected to the source. If you are not sure of what you are doing, do not take on the demon. It will awaken in you your deepest fears and the threshold of psychic torture it will put you through might overtake your ability to absorb and transform. You must be centered.

All around us there is a whirling of activity by the angels who have to work full time to protect humanity. If you think things are bad now, imagine if the angel substrata was not there. All of those near misses would be hits. Speak with them and begin to see when the air becomes a little wavy. The corner of your eye detects motion. Eventually with practice your vision will become increasingly clear. Angels are not rare at all; they are everywhere. Archangels overseeing the astral plane can only be contacted when you are ready to look them in the eye.

This is not a mythology but a guide for practice. See for yourself if it is true. If not, this hard core empty 3D world is but a prison and we are all being punished for something we didn't do. Thank God that this is not the case. It is a mystical world of wonder that goes higher and higher and higher. Beings upon beings and everything we have dreamed has a place somewhere. We as omnipotent humans can interact with anything anywhere anytime we'd like. Learn what you can become.

Once you liberate your spirit and remember your full story, you are ready to take your place in the world as an awakened being responsible for what you create around you. No longer letting life simply happen to you, you will stand up and with keen ability to manifest your vision you will build the future brick by brick. The limited dogmas pertaining only to the flesh are raised even as the many extensions of each fractal. There are subtler layers superimposed upon the rigid ones. A major chord becomes a minor 7th, which becomes a #11. Colors are not only RED and ORANGE, but each of the ever changing hues of fire.

Oppression can not exist where you exist. Influence can not abide in the presence of the self-aware. Share this power. Find ways to encode this precious knowledge everywhere. Let the roots keep growing and nurture them with your attention and time. Love yourself, Love Life, and Love the Changes that are even now expressing the Tao.

Jesus through Christ Consciousness

Jesus didn't have any friends who understood him. With the women he could always speak the language of woman. The men were too simple and uneducated to grasp abstract meanings.

Jesus resonated the Love of the Holy Spirit and Saved (retrieved) Souls. The teaching of the Essenes was very Shaman like. Most minds are not developed enough to receive the mystery.

Jesus did have fear; he was also in full surrender. Consciously serving the will of the Creator he walked forward. Accepting the outside while embracing inner nature, he demonstrated wholeness.

Jesus carried the cross while the people spat upon him. T is for truth; faith in truth is what the cross represents. The hardest part of the crucifixion was the unrealized potential.

Angel Buddha Christopher: Cosmic Ambassadors of Joy

"To be back in a place where I can once again somehow deliver a communication to the people of Earth is both a pleasure and a necessity. Gliding away is not an option until certain things have come to pass. I could disappear, but it is not often that one finds such clarity and meets it with the ability to express the intricacies of spirit. Bumping up against mind filters, we have to find a way to slip a little Truth into the deeper reaches of our inner realm. It takes but one ray of light to dissipate darkness. O seekers, heed the eternal call! Let not the undulations of the world hold sway. The ephemeral can be enjoyed and experienced, but one must never believe that they belong within it, because if they do, when the changes turn the present into the past, their concept of self will be battered against the rocks on the shore of time to be lost forever.

Watch out for thought loops. They will catch you and cause you to repeat the same foolish mistakes that have been occurring on the blue-green planet for millennia. Masters demonstrating self-awareness are rare gems who have appeared through/in time to keep the fires of realization stoked. It makes one shed a tear for their beauty and imagination. While most people go about their tiny lives, the sage basks in eternity, dropping fragrant rose pedals in hopes of perhaps stirring a memory. With humor and a twinkle of knowing, they sing the song of salvation from soul to soul. Using vibration they reinvigorate dead cells and cause them to once again dance. What could you do if every atom in your body was smiling? No longer simply a glorified eating-machine, you would find purpose in your nature and fulfillment from its expression.

You are slowly evolving out of your infancy as a species. Do not let EGO react in horror at the idea that you have not already arrived. Think in terms of millions of years and you will see that you have only recently emerged, and are just now starting to remember that you are more than the shell you are staying in. When we become aware of this, our inner light starts shining through the skin, changing the frequency of our resonance and merging the Body, Mind, Soul into one transcendent conscious entity. To drastically simplify simply for the sake of giving the living something to grasp onto regarding ascension, the Body is the 3rd dimension, the Mind when freed of identification with the body and when viewed from the Heart, is the 4th (Astral/Dream world), and the Soul reawakened, unified, in tune with the Sun, and now home, is the 5th.

You, spirit as flesh, are an interesting creation. Each manifestation brings something unique into the picture that everyone can benefit from. Building upon lessons already learned, the individual can avoid typical pitfalls on the path, and instead opt for an application of universal law in the support of good. This is why it is advisable to study history and to soak up information from those who have walked many roads. Assimilating all of it and rising above, humanity is moved forward in the only sensible way. So many pieces from so many places have come together in your body vehicle given as a gift from the Earth. Believe me, if She did not want you here, you would not be. He, the Sun, sends you Wisdom, and She sends you Love. Destiny awaits the cosmic ambassadors who will travel forth to share the Joy of your Solar System."

Angel Buddha Christopher Reaches out to Brad and Angelina

"It is not surprising that you have found each other. It is also not unexpected that you would have to dart around the globe to have the private romantic time that you both need. Brad, you should not feel bad at all for leaving Jennifer. You and Angelina have past life ties that made it inevitable that you would come together. You have fragments of Anthony and Cleopatra that to this day long to be close with overwhelming magnetism. This is also why there is an overtone of the forbidden around this coming together. It is part of the backdrop that makes the flames of passion burn even hotter. You are pulled out of this world into a timeless state of bliss.

You are ancient royalty and can not hide this fact because it clearly resonates. (For those who can see, Kobe Bryant has this energy as well.) Remember above all that this is a spiritual quality. Reflected in you is the ideal of living life as a god or goddess. This is an understanding that all of humanity can aspire to. It is also the way things were meant to be on Earth. People clamoring just to get a glimpse of you, is testimony to the madness of those who have not yet discovered their own divinity. Perhaps one day you will be able to turn to the crowd and use the opportunity to share some of the deeper lessons of life. If you were to open up in this way, people would listen.

Assimilate all you have experienced in this incarnation and all the lessons of your past lives. Take back up the soul's greater journey and move on. You will most likely one day remember that you are just visiting here; stars on Earth who come from the stars. Your cosmic heritage will provide many of the answers to the hidden aches in your heart. If centered in a growth process, your relationship will bear much fruit. Be cautious not to let old mind habits associated with others come to the fore and be shared one upon the other. Externalize in an atmosphere of acceptance and mutual understanding. It takes time, but soon the past will fade away and you can find new joy in each moment.

The highest achievement in existence is not fame, fortune, or fans. It is to become awakened to eternal truth. I send you blessings and good wishes for your nature to be set free."

Lennon – Revolution's Soldier

"You must never forget that before anything I was and am a soldier. The cause I fight for is Justice. Sure, Peace and Love and all that, but there will be no chance for it if humanity is crushed by the forces of oppression. You must see the beauty, and shout about the beast. If you'll notice by listening once more and yet again to the sutra music I left behind, I give rise to both in my vision. You must never get too light in the loafers about me and relegate me to yet another New Age-r who can not speak freely. That was one thing I grew to hate about the Beatles, what you call now, Political Correctness.

'Imagine' was one tune and not even my favorite. 'God' is better, 'O My Love' is better yet, and 'Revolution' among the best. It is easy to associate me with 'Imagine', but it is misleading to believe or promote that that alone was what I was or am all about. Look at my whole body of work….the progression…and let that be an indicator that helps you link to my spirit. This is the way to get to know me, and any of you can do it. Use my advice to transform your own view of the world. I am indicating a realm. You can join me here.

Do not let planted stories on the internet about me being a communist and such utter crap, allow you to be swayed. There are some human beings who are truly sincere and I was one of them. I bared my soul to all of you and demonstrated my spiritual progress to inspire you to do the same. I kept moving and still keep moving. I encourage you to do the same. Life keeps moving and so should we.

I know many still dream of the Beatles and color every word with their own hopes and perspective. John the man is far more than anything we used to be in the old days. When you find the truth, it is enough."

Horus the Hawk Head

"You have known me as many different faces in many different phases of your history. More recently in your societies, you have not seen us whom you used to love as anything but a footnote of antiquity. The religions that developed from the 'Old Testament' as you call it, have been like a fever that has gripped humanity and taken much from them. Simply being an old text does not give it any special significance. True, it is one account of humanity from an earlier time, but why do you not give Egyptian and Mesopotamian documents parity in your reckoning and ascriptions of value?

Your pre-history is rich in tradition and full of mysteries which you are only now starting to foray into. It is a shame that only so few read the cuneiform tablets that are available in plenty. How can you trust without your own verification through personal understanding? Eventually humanity should plug all ancient remnants into a massive computer database. Documents containing language should be decoded and made available for all to peruse. Getting to know the people through their expression, you can re-

link to the culture and open the doorway to the
wisdom they embodied.

For centuries I was prominent in the affairs of
Humanity. Pharaohs followed my model. True
there is a One-ness that underlies all of Existence,
but that does not preclude the possibility of Life
throughout higher dimensions. Herein lies the
great error in your modern
philosophical/spiritual reasoning. In most of the
standard traditions there is a leap to the extreme
and a denial of astral possibilities. Some, like the
Egyptians of Old, and their ancestors in the
Pleiadian area of the Universe were aware of the
Body, Oneness, and the hierarchy of entities in
between.

I am a Son of God. Some of what you have
worshipped in Christ is really a prayer to me. For
these Love vibrations I thank you. Jesus Christ is
a different type of God man. He brings Spirit
down to the people and delivers it on their terms.
This never was my choice as I prefer to rein
Supreme. The hawk quality is often associated
with me as I am a god of Awareness, servant of
the Eye. So to be precise I am the Son of the Sun.
Though I may have receded from the mind of
man, my contribution to human development

will echo throughout your continued evolution.

We will talk again when you remember your life beyond the handful of incarnations under the influence of your Mother the Earth. She is an embodiment of a yet higher entity – Kali/Isis. With unimaginable power and beauty, Woman slides through all the realms. A monument to this quality and an anchor for the feminine energies, the Statue of Liberty in your American harbor is no different than many of the wonders of the Ancient World. Today she holds steady even under the strain that is currently superimposing itself over your land. Help Her help you to remain free."

The Great Milky Way Black Hole

Just as the expression of Creation is analogous to the exhale of a breath, so too the Great Milky Way Black Hole is the Inhale for the vastness that is the body of our Galaxy.

The only reason your conduit is able to interpret this is because the Great Black Hole re-reversed the messages and brought them to a place that could be understood in the Earth planet's vernacular. Further translations to reach all who can be reached are up to others who will follow their divinely inspired inner inclination.

"Some of you are in danger of losing a grip on reality. Taking the conspiracy and the heavenly realizations too far, you have constructed an alternate and more complex matrix. Seeing your way back from this edge will be almost impossible if you are left to continue proving yourself right. Truth never feels like a fever. You will know who among you is aware because they are relaxed, good humored, and they listen. Seek them out and be with them.

Black holes are rejuvenators; giant tornadic vacuum cleaners that sweep space of all dissipating energy and turn it back around through the stars. Imagine the whole Universe with the stars as exhales (Shakti) and the black holes as inhales (Shiva); one gargantuan living entity warbling an ever-morphing plethora of realities.

There is more, but for now this will do."

Secrets of the Galaxy

Secrets of the Galaxy I: Sirius gets Serious

"As an elder in this part of the Galaxy, I would like you to know a little more about your Sun from my perspective. You could almost consider me an Uncle to your Sun, therefore a Great Uncle to you. Your Sun, though brilliant, would be considered about a teenager to speak in Human terms. He has some amazing thoughts, and we are very pleased with His Creative work for the most part. You may have noticed the phenomenon of solar flares and how they are increasing? Well, these could be considered emotional growing pains the Sun is having and unfortunately it is having a distinct and profound impact on your mother Gaia, and upon life on Earth.

Things will be okay and we are here to give the Sun, your father, Love and assistance in His own transformation. Through and beyond these temporary darker overtones is a higher consciousness for the Sun and this is being transferred into the open hearts of Humans on Earth. You are for the first time being given the capability to sync up completely with your father. His thoughts will be yours and we the

Stars in the Galaxy can then communicate directly to you all. Many of you are destined to go even farther when all lessons have been learned in your Solar System. There are many other star systems and planets with so many experiences to have!

I have been in contact with Humanity often in the past. The Atlanteans knew me, the Egyptians knew me, the Greeks knew me, and many native peoples were blessed by my deep ancient wisdom. Would you not think that many would say hello to the brightest star in your sky? I am always communicating with you. All of us stars have voices. Learn again to listen to the messages we have never stopped transmitting. You fill your precious subtle minds with such static. Get away from the artificial lights and break free from the background noise. Get back to Life in Nature and see things as they were in the beginning, for each day this eternal truth is born anew.

It is such a pleasure to transmit this message. We have been following the ascension process many of you are going through and are greatly encouraged to see you building such fast and steady friendships with each other. Keep the faith and stand strong together in what you are doing. It is the right direction and the way the awakening miracle is going to occur on your planet. Light is expanding in every direction. One person reaches another and another and another. Soon you will be shining stars in your own right and you will take your place next to us in space. So many blessings are afforded the living. I am sure you and I will be friends for thousands of years."

Secrets of the Galaxy II: Rigel's Revelations

"From my unique position in Orion I have been able to see a lot of what you humans on Earth might call Juicy Galactic Gossip. Again and again I have watched as those lizards cruise by on the way to give you a visit and tinker with your DNA. One thing they want to do is reemphasize medulla power and strangle the creative energies that arrive through the higher parts of the brain. Hammering on the humans they have been able to dull many by pushing the soul right out of the body. Thinking only in terms of security and survival, the darkness of fear activates the repressions in many and locks them in on themselves. Cut off from the Source, their Soul begins to suffocate and die.

De-evolution to the instinctual animal is being resisted by light workers who are desperately attempting to wake sensitive people up. Showing the people how to heal and reclaim their individual power is what they were sent to Earth to do. They come from other parts of the Galaxy such as the Pleiadian and Andromedan areas of Space. Many beings from many frequencies are on the Earth at this time. From where I am, you can see them arrive, and then dive into the portal of incarnation. Human bodies are the vehicles for travel on Earth; they in no way indicate the greater continuity of your being. Your energy body remembers what it is like to fly through the Stars.

You would not have been allowed to enter the Earth experience unless you were in some way prepared for it. Normally you think in terms of your Earthly existence being Life, and death being the end of it. From where I am, it looks like you are orbiting the Earth and keep swooping in for a closer look...to enjoy the fruits of the Garden. There are some among your company that hang out high above the others, silently watching over them. They operate at greater time intervals and drop in on occasion to assist in the progressing of events. They also counteract some of the lower level demon influences that continue to nag humanity due to the suppressed emotional states of most people.

It is a joy to see that some humans are beginning to peal away the limitations of 5 sense perception and open up the secret surprise that was always inside. You are so close to evolving to the next stage of your species' destiny. Some of you are already there and so make it easier for the others.

Even as Buddha arrived home and Jesus opened a gate for the Sons and Daughters of God, so too each of you who attains to realization makes it that much easier for the others because you are all connected and the raising of one's vibrations raises all others. We stars always send you supportive energy. You dream when you gaze upon us, because the wonder that is awakened is your own Soul potential.

Remember Rigel as your friend. You can communicate with me anytime day or night. It is easy if you believe you can do it and are patient enough to establish the link. Even if we resonate silently together, we can share many journeys through the Universe. I will do what I can to facilitate your transformation. I will introduce you to the other stars that I know and we will always be together as a family. I Love you. Open up your Heart to receive my gifts and brilliantly we will shine as One. There will be more stories another day, and until that time, I wish you well and look forward to all things that are potential becoming actual. The game goes on and things are starting to turn in your favor."

Secrets of the Galaxy III: Vega's Vibes

"I have found my way into humanity's imagination with my gentle but persistent intent driven vibes. Being so close, I have often whispered sweet starlight into your ear. Life comes in many forms my friends. It isn't all in bodies. Consciousness, Intelligence, and Awareness exist throughout the galaxy in many different ways. Sometimes they exist as pure presence, and sometimes they are available for telepathic conversation. This is something you really must get used to. It is quite natural, and easier than you might preconceive.

If you would only consider that your own light body is made of stars, it wouldn't be so difficult for you to understand, that we, your star brothers and sisters, can interact with you. Some seem to allow for the possibility of influence by the planets in their own solar system, but many haven't yet considered deeply that all of the stars in the sky influence each other. Just because at the present in the body, you are smaller and there are many of you, doesn't mean that anything has changed. It is a great congregation, and if you could get along, anything would be possible.

Humanity intuits its own greatness underneath all the temporary eruptions of doubt and insanity. What if I told you that we've talked many times before? You just don't quite remember it yet because of that whole thing about losing your greater continuity when pressed into the Earth travel unit. You magnificent creatures have to back away from those 5 senses once in awhile and just feel the brilliance of your light. With your chakras stars you are a constellation yourself. Even more magical, you are walking around creating the myth right now!

Some of you will visit me in spirit and some in the human body in future incarnations. Some of you can reach me now if you drop a line from your 3rd eye. I'm always here and I always answer my calls. To the sailors and those who know the stars and use them to chart a true course through life, I send my thanks and best wishes. Often I send a bit of extra energy to encourage your bravery in the most dangerous of journeys. Humans are fascinating creatures, and I do Love you all. Gaze upon me and perhaps you will notice that I am looking back. "

Secrets of the Galaxy 4: Antares, Heart of the Scorpion

"Even as the human body takes on the form of your character, so too does the color and brightness of a star reflect the qualities of the being exuding this energy. Wake up to the truth that conscious life is all around you and your progress as a species has been observed since your conception. I'm not one of the nicest of stars in the sky but I am one of the most intense. There is much you can learn from me. With passion and depth of purpose, my thoughts contribute to structures that manifest throughout the Galaxy. Your thoughts can do the same when you are able to stand behind a vision and continue to work towards its realization. Experiments and failures are the path to success.

Ease yourself out of Time and you will find more happiness. Humans can never find peace until they are able to give up rushing around after unrealistic dream projections. From here it looks as if people are dizzy and keep tripping into obstacles they put in their own way. There are a few that come up to the sky for a breath of space. It is a whole different way of perceiving life in the Universe. If you are living against the clock, your time will run out; if you are living fully in the present, time does not apply. The more of 'You' is Here, the more will be experienced and the slower time will seem to move until one day you link into the flow of Aum through Existence and you are no more separate.

The Creator Source has a heartbeat which you and I both echo in our own pulsing nature. Creation is an ongoing masterwork that relies on cyclical rejuvenation. Creativity is a Holy wind breathing Life into matter...spirit into flesh. The rawness of Fire rips ignorance and the gentleness of the butterfly awakens imagination. No matter how many ways we characterize the Kingdom, it remains elusive to definition by always opening new portals. Like Existence, you too must open new portals. Your light is becoming too potent to keep in a jar anymore. You must give it room to shine or the compression will get greater and greater. You'll see when you can breathe again and a song arises from the depths of your soul.

It would be tremendously helpful to humans if they could learn to develop the quality of Intimacy. They have harmed each other so much in their money games that trust is hesitant and for most takes much time. The purity of Life on Earth would have Humanity openly trusting each other and revealing the depths of their inner world freely without fear of condemnation and judgment. Each individual can find this place and live this way. If for some reason you are betrayed it has no effect because trust is an aspect of being not a behavior. In fact compassion can arise for the betrayer and the hurt they must be carrying. Inspire this quality in others by daring to live so insightfully and uninfluenced by passing storms.

The strength of a sword rings from its sheath. Save offensive strikes until absolutely necessary then strike completely. There are times in nature where one must push back. Struggle is part of what made you humans what you have become. Since most of you have protection for your bodies, the struggle has moved to your minds. If you could let this go and remember yourselves as the transcendent beings that traveled to this area of the Universe for a learning vacation, you would be able to solve your worldly problems near instantly. There is no lack of solutions, only a lag in societal evolution. We can see that it is slowly coming along. Many lights have become brighter, but huge groups have gotten darker as well.

You bright folks (who will be the more likely to receive this transmission) should consider building your own space ships. From here it is obvious that the clouds will clear up and Venus will host another Eden. Mars civilization was destroyed, but the seeds made it to Earth. The Adam and Eve project specimens joined with the native inhabitants of Earth and were able to survive, and eventually thrive. The Earth's vibrations soothed the troubled souls that began incarnating and it seemed as if Earth would be the place for you all to heal. Then the OUTSIDE INFLUENCE occurred and early behavior patterns were reawakened causing humanity to veer wildly off developmental course.

You were supposed to be moving out into the Solar System by now. Your few probes are a meager extension of your eyes and ears. Many of you have dreams of going farther. This is possible. Become aware of the higher realms and bring this in when considering how to deal with the future. Adapt what you see in Existence to the tools you have at your disposal to create artifacts in harmony with the Tao. Then you will have efficiency and beauty. It is not often that I get to speak to humans with human words and I am satisfied that we have touched upon a few of the deeper realms. Many of you have communicated telepathically with me before and a couple of you knew me before this incarnation. I was once a marvelous giant planet much like your Jupiter and Saturn if merged as one and twice the size. I orbited the grandest of stars Helicon..."

Secrets of the Galaxy 5 – Grandpa Betelgeuse

"Stars eventually leave their old bodies to have new and greater experiences even as humans do. I am currently in the protracted process of slipping out of the red supergiant that you see in Orion's shoulder and have called Betelgeuse. When I have fully escaped and the blooming of the lotus of my life in this vehicle for expression unfolds, you will see a supernova flash across your sky screen. Even from your small planet Earth it will be an extremely noteworthy event. At this time, all I have learned will be released and those that are receptive will feel a tremendous influx of energy.

Having known most of the beings in this area of the Milky Way since they were born, I am relating in the manner that you humans might call 'grandfather' to those around me. Much of my energy is retreating inwards, but I still keep half an eye open to what is being created in the space around me. Sometimes I even have a look towards humanity to see if there is anyone I can have a chat with. I am always up for a cosmic tea party. What we share does not have to be of the most ultimate nature. Many of the stars go on and on about the Source and when they communicate with humans, they are always bringing the conversation to a knife's edge.

I've been through so much that it is nice to simply be here and say hello. Intensity has its proper place and that is why the younger stars are naturally driven to manifest this in the necessary ways. After watching so many things occur, you develop a distance in your perspective. This inner space makes relaxation possible because no matter what happens, part of me is not involved. If you can learn a talent from me regarding how to approach your life, this would be it. As a silent observer, you are present, you reflect things exactly as they are, and you do not surrender part of your being to passing phenomenon.

Let me take you on my celestial knee for a moment. Sweet star children, the Universe is a marvelous place! Never forget that you belong amongst the stars and that the whole Existence is your home. You are never alone, you just sometimes feel like you are. Remember that we have always been here and always will be in some form. Seasons change, and many things rise and fall. The Love that brings two friends together never fades away. It has been my pleasure for us to connect. I shall never forget you and I pray that you remember me."

Secrets of the Galaxy 6: Polaris and Friends

"I have guided many a seeker before and will continue to do so for some time. Eventually I will be released from your eyes as Pole Star designation and shall be just another star in your sky. I look forward to the quiet, and am already experiencing the winding down of attention in my direction. Even a couple of hundred years ago, many humans were connecting with me nightly. Sharing energy, they came to look upon me as an old friend. Some developed a relationship with me that lasted through many Earth lives. How much humanity has forgotten! They wind their way forward at a reckless pace, convinced that they are advancing, not remembering that the whole point of the journey was supposed to be to discover and enjoy.

Being quite a distance from your Sun's System, it is a marvel that communication can be successfully established. Human beings are a wonder. Throughout your species' existence, many have shown the propensity towards remarkable perceptions and achievements. I honor you and have learned from you even as you have from me. Perhaps you may not be

117

consciously aware of my influence, but over the years, I have guided humanity not just as a marker in the sky, but as an archetypal representation of an aspect of your subconsciousness; something in you which is unswayed no matter how difficult the journey. Sailing a straight and steady course with your life, you can never go wrong.

I'd like you to know Merak and Dubhe. They have been humbly silent, but are feeling forlorn simply being seen by modern man as the stars that point to me. As a friend to humanity, I ask you to enjoy them on their own terms the next time you see them in the sky. One of those nights when the big dipper looms enormously overhead, cast your eyes upon the last two stars and thank them for their beauty. For them I have much gratitude. They have been good friends to me and I wish to share their blessed qualities with you. In the greater bear they make up part of the mother to the lesser bear child of which I am a part. Centuries of human stories are derived from existential truths that have been intuitively perceived."

(Merak and Dubhe come forward.)

"Our Love for Polaris brought us to add in this joyous expression. How inconceivable it was for us to have this means of communication where we can speak to humans in human language. Of course we always interact light upon light, but this method develops the intimacy so the next time you see us in the sky we will have a deeper connection and the energy dance of our auras will mean more. We could each speak individually but in this moment prefer to unify and say that we are here in friendship. Honored to portray an aspect of the Great Bear, we have warmth and regard for all of life. We are gentle, lucid, and would like to mention that Polaris is not the Pole star by coincidence. It takes a certain kind of leader even amongst the stars to hold the attention of millions through millennia. Without a bit of angst, this noble sentinel has a unique quality that has steadily held together the center of our mythos."

(Polaris returns…)

"I will hold forth for some time and after awhile recede to give another the duty of maintaining core vigilance. Imagine all the stars pulsing while they converse with one another. There is much chatter in the skies. If only you knew! Many stars gossip about one another even like human teenagers. This might seem odd until you remember that all is God playing with God. There are so many ways for Existence to experience itself and all of our forms, disguises, roles, and masks, are just colors of the game. Above all relieve yourself of worry, guilt, and unnecessary stress. The process of letting go is a path that will never lead you astray. Find your own center and stay the course."

Secrets of the Galaxy 7: Gentle Deneb

"In the Swan I am the tail and in the Northern
Cross, I am the head of Christ.   As part of the
Summer Triangle, I, Vega and Altair remind you
of the divine power of 3. Simply gaze through
the portal we create, open up and allow
perceptions to form. This is a type of dimensional
gateway for higher energies to flow into this area
of space. Imagine a steady stream of Love
pouring through. You can drink of this and be
healed of any ailment. Relaxing you can touch
the present more deeply than ever before.

I have successfully been able to cultivate an area
of peacefulness in my sphere of influence for
many millennia. A combination of vigilance and
compassion has created a celestial oasis that many
galaxian races have silently acknowledged is one
place where they will not war. An aspect of why
my method has worked is because it is free of
judgment. This allows others to be non-
differentiating as well in my presence. It is the
harmony of the center revealed from without,
encouraging the process within.

Along the path of the Milky Way, many come
here to be in the quietly rejuvenating energies

that emanate from my being. Any can partake of this resonant energy anytime. I can tell the facilitator of this message even now is deepening his connection to my subtle soothing vibes. Most beings who find their way to your solar system have been here before. For the destructive aspects of some of these beings, I am aware and would like you to know that I know about what has been occurring.

At the core of my message to you is to see yourself as you are and recognize the beauty of it. So many create an idea about what they would like to be and constantly feel that they are failing to live up to what they themselves have constructed. Then they suffer self condemnation and the agony of guilt. Cycling downward deeper and deeper into the prison, it takes a mighty lifeline to save the day. Acceptance of the uniqueness of each creature speaks to reason as well as feeling which awakens understanding.

You must also realize that you are swimming through the air even as the Aquatics on your planet swim through water. Is it not clear to you yet that you emerged from the Sea? This is the womb of the Earth. There is much about your world that you know about only in ancient myths and fairytales. Thank the Creator that you have this much or else you would have no link at all to reconnect with what is still there and more. All the beings in all the realms are aware of and experiencing the same transition that are you humans.

I am your friend and my light always shines in support of your efforts towards transformation."

Secrets of the Galaxy 8: Pleiadian Echoes

"One of the strongest influences on your Earth culture, we know all there is to know about you. Where we exist, time does not move as it does for you. A million years is like a moment. Your growth as a species can easily be considered in a scientific manner. Your planet looks remarkably like a Petri dish to us sometimes. The difference is in those among you who have been able to consciously connect to their own source. They transcend the circumstance and are capable of communication with the greater universe.

We have always and always will send you vibrations of harmony. At various times, our aesthetic has come to the forefront of human affairs and things have been peaceful for many years. The Atlantians and later the Egyptians were well acquainted with our mysteries. You see echoes of our presence in the hieroglyphs and depictures of ancient god forms. Imagine silence deepening and penetrating every bit of space. Release boundaries of thought and interpretation. Just be and let pure presence remain.

Each of you is much like our star cluster many call the 7 sisters. Each individual star maintains independence while working together for the good of all. So the 7 becomes 1. Now this new unity can take part in an even greater community. In like manner, each of your 7 chakras is 1, representing a world of its own. When they work together, the 7 becomes 1. Then this higher 1 can work with other 1's here to become yet another level of organic oneness. This is the way dimensions are superimposed upon one another and transmigrated.

Eventually all stars will unite to serve truth. There are just a few lost in bodies that have forgotten the Joy of Unity. They will suffer for awhile; perhaps may even cycle through a few more incarnations. Not to worry. Purity is being restored in your area. Sol has had enough of the Free Will experiment careening forward unimpeded; it has been thrown off by outside influence. He can turn a deaf ear to Gaia's pleas no longer. Harmony must be established in a way that reflects the growth of experience and the beauty of nature."

Secrets of the Galaxy 9: Aldebaran, Eye of the Bull

"Coming forward to speak out of necessity, I reinforce certain aspects of character that have been somewhat lacking in humanity's display of attributes as of late. Know ye no sense of honor or integrity? So ready to trade away self-respect for fleeting gain, people are destroying their own souls for what amounts to absolutely nothing in time. One must focus on the eternal not the transitory. Up and down are merely the oscillations that bring beings to understanding through experience. You must remember to bravely play the cosmic game. Rather than searching for final victory, enjoy the intricacy of its unfolding.

Choices made with the whole Earth community in mind will awaken the nobler qualities in humanity that had unfortunately grown dormant through the instigation and repetition of lesser brain pathways. Beware of that which constantly draws you out through the senses. Pleasurable at first, many of these enticements can become addictions which pull you again and again down from spirit consciousness into solely body perception. Rather than living in the open free

127

spaces of the inner world, you will be always in search of sensation. One of your Souls, Gautama Buddha, was a pioneer of freedom in this regard.

Throughout history I have been associated with the Bull's Eye and have also been recognized as an emissary for Archangel Michael. Indeed today He is more active in the Earth sphere than He has been for millennia, due largely to the fact that certain dark forces were set loose by mischievous entities. This is all part of the cosmic cycles and provides the circumstance where angelic beings can become more personally involved with humanity's spiritual progression. Truly this is a time of great joy for those on the astral plane. They understand that it is the backdrop of darkness which makes light possible.

It is the right moment to call forth your own personal power and engage in the effort to protect and encourage the children of light. They must come to understand that it is not unloving to protect yourself from one who harms you. The perpetrator may immediately polarize and try to define you, but that is the only technique they have, and once you learn to hold steadfast in spite of their reproaches, they will no longer have any control over you. Often the demonic entities attempt to evoke your worst fears, but if you have taken over this process consciously, they will find themselves rendered completely impotent.

Be truthful, be strong, and be well good spirits. I send you the benefit of my energy always."

CREATIVECOSMOS.ORG

Mission of the Creative Cosmos

To invoke the unity of Eastern Wisdom and Western Art.

To assist in the evolving consciousness and destiny of humanity.

To make this information available to the widest possible audience.

http://www.creativecosmos.org

www.ingramcontent.com/pod-product-compliance
Lightning Source LLC
Chambersburg PA
CBHW072022040426
42447CB00009B/1686